T0194644

Discovering
a New Beginning

A Journey in Remarriage

AARON L. GRAVETT

WESTBOW
PRESS®
A DIVISION OF THOMAS NELSON
& ZONDERVAN

WestBow Press books may be ordered through booksellers or by contacting:

WestBow Press
A Division of Thomas Nelson & Zondervan
1663 Liberty Drive
Bloomington, IN 47403
www.westbowpress.com
1 (866) 928-1240

ISBN: 978-1-9736-6662-2 (sc)
ISBN: 978-1-9736-6663-9 (hc)
ISBN: 978-1-9736-6661-5 (e)

Library of Congress Control Number: 2019908875

Print information available on the last page.

WestBow Press rev. date: 10/15/2019

To my Lord and Savior, Jesus Christ, for without Him I am nothing. And to my lady, my best friend and wife, Sheila. She is truly my gift of grace from Christ. God has used her powerfully in my life, and I can never thank Him enough for her. She amazes me with her persistence in life's challenges and her faithfulness with everything God has placed before her. I love her with all my heart—always and forever.

Contents

Foreword

Divorce is messy, emotional, and painful. It strips you of all you are and leaves you exposed to the world and their judgments. It presents an array of emotions and a sense of loss to navigate as you step forward, with trepidation, on your path of life. Then there's the religious sect. You may have tried to reenter their world and found yourself wondering where you fit in—or if you ever will fit in.

Colliding with all the external perceptions is the internal battle that rages. Questions crash against your soul constantly: How does God see you now? Are you still loved by Him? Has He abandoned you? Can He ever forgive you and accept you again?

In this book, *Discovering a New Beginning*, Pastor Aaron does an excellent job calming your fears and exposing the misconceptions of divorce using the truth of scriptures. For, you see, grace and love go farther than a divorce decree. God's love for you is truly unconditional, without bounds, eternal.

Pastor Aaron has taken his experiences as a divorcee and a remarried man, who has lived the heartache and rejection of the church and then rediscovered God's grace through a second marriage, and carefully penned words to teach healing and peace, as the words of truth have brought for him.

The wisdom found on the pages of this book can lead you to freedom. First, from within as you draw closer to Christ, discovering the love and healing He has for you. Then, freedom from the opinions of others, learning to live beyond wrong teaching in the church, discovering divorce doesn't mean death to your walk with Christ—serving, worshipping, ministering, fulfilling the call of the Lord on your life. Truly, in all that we live through in this life, we can learn and grow closer to the Lord and then help others with the same love and compassion the Lord gave us when we faced the circumstance.

Pastor Aaron does an excellent job helping you navigate a new marriage and discovering your new spouse in a manner that enables you to love the way God intended for you to love. This is the way Christ has led and taught Aaron to love through His Word. If you apply these principles, though not always easy, as it requires us to get over ourselves, you will truly discover and embrace your new beginning. A new beginning not only with your new spouse but most importantly with Christ.

Thank you, Pastor Aaron, for writing a book that is needed for healing. A voice that has risen to speak truth. I pray the voice of truth in this book reaches the hurting and brings healing. I pray it opens the eyes of ministers who have wrongly divided scripture and belittled divorcees, treating them as second-class Christians who were not fit for the work of the church. I pray it strengthens marriages and brings Christ to the center of them so they will never be broken. May each person who reads this come to know Jesus as they have never known Him before and be stronger in their faith and love for Him. May the truth of this book reach many for years to come.

Sheila Gravett

Introduction

They say you should always write about what you know. The first thing I want to say is that I never saw myself writing a book on remarriage. I never thought, *You know, one day I want to get divorced so that I can write on remarriage.* Divorce happens though, and whether or not it was your fault, many—and I mean many—people find themselves divorced and wondering, *Now what?*

Life seems to be all turned around, and you question everything in your life, even your own salvation. The two of you were "one flesh," and then suddenly it seems like you're half a person. Your whole life is turned upside down.

This is not a book on divorce though; it is a book on remarriage—discovering a new beginning. This subject is taboo for most in the church because they don't study scripture enough to see what it says; therefore, they treat divorced and remarried people as second-class Christians. They treat them as saved but as failures at the same time.

The great news is just as Christ is the God of second (or more) chances for life, He is the God who gives it for love as well. There is a new beginning, and the greatest love you could ever have might be about to walk into your life. So whether you think you could love again, you just found your new love, you just got remarried, or you have been remarried for a long time, this book is for you.

I am going to take the blinders off and make it clear through this journey of discovery with me. I am not perfect in my marriage (my lady can vouch for that). I have made plenty of mistakes, said words I wished I could grab back, and even made her cry, which I truly hate. Yet I know that, with Christ's help, He can build anyone up in Him and in the process make a new journey beautiful.

I won't be presenting other people's situations—only my own. You won't read quotes upon quotes from other people's books and articles. We have enough books out there that are only rehashes of other people's work. You, the reader, need to know that the words you are reading come from a person who has been there and done that. I will speak from experience, using the Word of God combined with practical advice to show you how to traverse the amazing, thrilling, and intense adventure of remarriage.

I will also be using scripture passages that will appear in multiple chapters, since the theme of these passages can be interwoven through many aspects of remarriage. The use of scripture is of utmost importance, since God is the creator and sustainer of the Christian life and marriage.

In this book, we will cover the challenges, rewards, obstacles, and different parts of the journey that will make this marriage the best and last one. This love is your God-given love of a lifetime!

Chapter One

God Didn't Divorce You

It All Starts with a Death

The day came when it happened. The sun was out, and the sky was a dark blue. I probably would have noticed how beautiful it was if my world had not been crashing down all around me. I was standing in the driveway watching my life end, it seemed. When the vehicle was just out of sight, the sorrow overwhelmed me to the point I could hardly breathe. The tears of sorrow welled up to the point that I mourned heavily. I couldn't stand upright but doubled over sobbing. To this day, I don't know how long I stood there mourning, but I know the tears finally stopped falling. When I finally stood straight again, I was a broken man.

So many people call divorce "a living death." You really don't understand the gravity of that statement until you go through one. Whether the divorce was the other person's fault or it was your own fault, whether the divorce happened to you or you were the one to divorce the other, it still feels like a living death.

The first thing I want to point out is that I believe with all my heart what the Bible says, which is that God is against divorce. Scripture is very plain on this.

But from the beginning of the creation God made them male and female. For this cause shall a man leave his father and mother, and cleave to his wife; and they twain shall be one flesh: so then they are no more twain, but one flesh. What therefore God hath joined together, let not man put asunder. (Mark 10:6–9)

Staying together is the perfect will of God. If you are reading this book and divorce has not happened yet, I encourage you to seek God through prayer, the Word of God, the advice of your pastor, and, if need be, a Christian counselor. Do everything in your power to seek reconciliation and healing. This book is written, though, for those who for one reason or another have found themselves on the other side of the divorce that has already happened.

The pain of a divorce can be unbearable. The loneliness can set in to such an extreme extent that there will be times you will cry until there are no tears left. Sad to say, some have experienced the absence of the spouse, the children, the extended family, the friends, and even the Christian brothers and sisters as they felt that they had to choose a side.

This is a natural behavior because divorce in the public's eye always has a victim and an evil monster whose fault it was. I hate to break this to the Christian world, but every person in a divorce is a victim because the devil only wants to destroy, and divorce is one of his biggest weapons.

You know exactly what I'm talking about. You have experienced this pain. You have experienced the separation of everyone you seem to know, and you may even now feel the heavens are brass. The closeness you once had with Jesus Christ now seems to be just a memory. So what do you do?

The first thing is to concentrate on the restoration of yourself. This is difficult because you feel that you need to concentrate on all the external things, such as getting a new residence if you're the one who was asked to leave, missing the spouse and the children, court, child support, and a host of other things that bombard you.

For you to come out with a vibrant relationship with Christ, though, the first step—and one that needs to permeate your every day—is to concentrate on Jesus Christ, who still loves you more than any other and is still with you in the trenches. Listen to this: whether it was your fault or not, in Christ, there is always forgiveness. In most divorces, each person has blame. There is usually blame to share, but there is no sense reliving that over and over. The time to concentrate on is the here and now. Christ promises forgiveness for all who seek His forgiveness and repent.

> *If we confess our sins, he is faithful and just to forgive us our sins, and to cleanse us from all unrighteousness. (1 John 1:9)*

That is one awesome promise of God right there! Before reading more of this book, stop, slowly read that verse again, and commit to believe and obey it. Let the forgiveness of Christ sweep over you and give you a breath of fresh air to sweep the sin and the guilt right out of your life.

Once again, divorce feels like a living death, but realize that when you are in Christ and you keep your faith in Him, you are still in life no matter how the circumstances may feel around you.

> *In him was life; and the life was the light of men. (John 1:4)*

The fact that you need to get deep into your heart and soul is this: Jesus Christ is still with you!

When you are feeling alone, and people are separating from all around you, hold on to the fact that Christ will never leave you or forsake you! (Read Hebrews 13:5.)

That is a promise He made in His Word to you. If you are

honest, though, when you are going through such a thing as a divorce, in the months leading up to it, it can be hard for you to pray and read the Word of God. The sad truth is the very thing we usually give up is the very thing that God wants us to do even more. He still desires intimacy with us.

Read this verse and realize God's plan for you, as opposed to what the enemy of your soul wishes for you:

> *The thief cometh not, but for to steal, and to kill, and to destroy: I am come that they might have life, and that they might have it more abundantly. (John 10:10)*

Let's break down this verse within the context of a divorce. When divorce happens, the first thing the enemy does is steal the intimacy and affection of the relationship. The specialness that seemed to ignite when you looked at each other is gone, and it feels like someone stole it. His next thing is to kill the closeness of the relationship, which will cause the relationship to be destroyed. This is not God's plan; it is God's will that divorce doesn't happen and the relationship is restored.

This book addresses the situation in which you are on the other side of the divorce and no reconciliation of the marriage can be obtained. The enemy has already stolen, killed, and destroyed. Now he wants you to live defeated.

This is when, no matter what, you ask God to help you believe that the second part of that verse is still for you. Christ still wants you to have life in Him and have it more abundantly, even after divorce. Unlike what many in society and some in the church say, God does not throw you away.

The first step is to take the first step. Get alone with Christ in prayer and His Word and reestablish that close relationship with Him.

Christ Will Equip and Help You
Every Step of the Way

*Grace and peace be multiplied unto you through
the knowledge of God, and of Jesus our Lord,
According as his divine power hath given unto
us all things that pertain unto life and godliness,
through the knowledge of him that hath called
us to glory and virtue. (2 Peter 1:2–3)*

The grace and power of God will be doing a work in you; in
fact, it is such a strong work that it is all you need for life and
godliness.

After the divorce, I didn't seek God as I should have. I
believed that God had given up on me and that, therefore, there
wasn't much of a point for me to work on being restored. I had
made some wrong choices, but I praise God that the Holy Spirit
was still convicting and bugging me the entire way. There was
also someone persisting in prayer for me as I went through this.
God heard those prayers, and I believe that is what kept the
Holy Spirit continuously in pursuit of me. Christ had saved me
and called me into ministry. Even though I was ready to give
it all up and even give up on myself, He had not forgotten me.

I also had no excuse. This passage declares that Christ has
given me His grace and His power. He has given unto me all
things for life and godliness through the knowledge of Him. It
was just time to surrender back to His plan, allow Him to pick
up the pieces and put them all together again. It was all up to
my "want to." If He sees your desire to want Him and His plans
in your life, then He will give you that same grace and power.

His equipping though is not some easy, fast-track, presto,
one-two-three-step process and you're done. Ah, shucks. I think
I may have busted a few bubbles! The reason is that every
person is different. What works for one person may not be what
another person needs. The activities you do in the Lord, though,
will bring about closeness to Christ, and in that process, He

will equip you for all that you need. The activities are and will always be prayer, study of God's Word, worship, and service.

Drawing closer in your relationship with Christ will be what He uses for you to realize He didn't divorce you. Let me add that you need to go deeper into Him and truly listen to His voice, because many voices around you, and even in the church, will keep you feeling like a second-class Christian. Focus instead on Him.

Let God Love on You First

Once again, divorce is hard, and it reaches down to the soul. It leads to countless nights in tears and days in confusion and numbness. Therefore, one of the most important things to do before you are remarried is to let God love on you first. Let Him heal and restore you. Even if you are already remarried, the healing of God can still take place in you now. The difference is once you are married again, you have the added benefit of allowing your new spouse to be used by God to help in that process. It can also be another aspect of bonding between the two of you.

Remember the love of God is vast.

> *Who shall separate us from the love of Christ? shall tribulation, or distress, or persecution, or famine, or nakedness, or peril, or sword? As it is written, For thy sake we are killed all the day long; we are accounted as sheep for the slaughter. Nay, in all these things we are more than conquerors through him that loved us. For I am persuaded, that neither death, nor life, nor angels, nor principalities, nor powers, nor things present, nor things to come, Nor height, nor depth, nor any other creature, shall be able to separate us from the love of God, which is in Christ Jesus our Lord. (Romans 8:35–39)*

No divorce can separate you from His love either. Praise God for that!

Understand, no study on remarriage is complete without an acknowledgment of why marriage is so special in the eyes of God. Too many people make the commitment of marriage to God and each other, but as soon as they want out, suddenly they minimize it to just a piece of paper. Realize this very deeply and let it sink in, because it will save your new marriage; a commitment to be married is a commitment for life, and it is a choice.

There are some churches that have changed the wedding vows to say, "As long as we both shall love." When I found that out, it just sickened me, because at any given time in a marriage, during a heated argument you may not feel love. With this mind-set, divorce is looming, and if your fiancé even considers this vow, run now ... and run fast! It means they are not committed to you right from the start.

Divorce is extremely difficult because of what God makes of a marriage commitment.

Therefore shall a man leave his father and his mother, and shall cleave unto his wife: and they shall be one flesh. (Genesis 2:24)

For this cause shall a man leave his father and mother, and cleave to his wife; And they twain shall be one flesh: so then they are no more twain, but one flesh. What therefore God hath joined together, let not man put asunder. (Mark 10:7–9)

When two people commit to marriage, they become one flesh. This means the marriage is now complete in such a unifying commitment to God that it is as if they are one person.

Even though each are still individuals, they now work as one unit, as one person. Therefore, when a divorce happens, it can leave a person feeling incomplete, as if they are half a person. Is it any wonder that healing is needed? For any wound, there needs to be mending. This mending takes some attention, relying on God for healing, and it's never to be ignored.

There are many people who try to skip this part, and it can cause more pain. Some, in the attempt to ignore and dull the pain, turn to things that won't work, such as quick relationships, work, hobbies, friends, drugs, alcohol, and illicit sex. Now, someone may read that and say that some of those things are not bad. But if you fill the void with quick relationships or even friendships, what happens when they end? What happens when the workplace turns sour (politics and fighting for promotions)? What happens when the hobby gets boring or you lose yourself in drugs, alcohol, or empty sex? Understand that none of those things will fill the void, and the reason is they aren't created to. The only one who can heal and completely fill the void is Jesus Christ. His love is eternal and powerful enough to handle your deepest wound and rawest pain.

Read Romans 8:35–39 again.

Christ's love is so powerful that it will cut through the pain, the hurt, the disappointment, and the numbness. That's not saying you won't feel the pain but that you will know and have the comfort that God will be with you through it.

Chapter Two

The Journey Ahead—A New Start Is Allowed

It's Going to Get Deep

Why do I say it's going to get deep? Well, simply put, most have never studied the principles of divorce and remarriage to know what the Word of God actually says about the subject.

So many voices will scream at you after the divorce, voices that will help and encourage but also voices of harm, condemnation, disappointment, and even total contempt. Unfortunately, many of those voices are from well-meaning believers. We will now look at the Bible and go through all the aspects and show that there can be a new start.

When I went through the divorce, I had voices mostly condemning the divorce, especially as a pastor. Then I had the added problem of fighting the traditional interpretation of some scripture passages when it came to the question of remarriage as a believer. I had the added negative voices on the concept of remarriage as a minister. It is my prayer that this chapter will provide answers to questions you may have. I pray you also allow the Word of God to cut through the voices that you hear so you can listen only to your Lord's voice.

Allow me to encourage you to sit down and read this whole

chapter in as much as one sitting as you can, so you can follow the flow that builds from one biblical passage to the next. I pray that you truly open your mind to the Holy Spirit as He reveals truth to you. This will answer your questions on the subject of divorce as well as help you show others accurate teaching.

Pastors and church leaders, if you are reading this, I encourage you to let these passages of God's Word shape what you believe on the subject. I also pray that you share it with those who have gone through the pain and tragedy of divorce to show them that there is still the hope of love.

So strap your seat belt on and let's dig. That's a saying, of course. Don't read and drive. That would be a bad thing!

The Biblical Reasons That God Allows for Divorce

> *It hath been said, Whosoever shall put away his wife, let him give her a writing of divorcement: But I say unto you, That whosoever shall put away his wife, saving for the cause of fornication, causeth her to commit adultery: and whosoever shall marry her that is divorced committeth adultery. (Matthew 5:31–32)*

Here we have a clear reason that God allows divorce: fornication of the offending party. When you look at this passage, it demonstrates that if not for this reason, even if one wrongly divorces another (besides for adultery), the offended party cannot remarry, or it would be committing adultery for the rest of their life.

This would be very dangerous, for 1 Corinthians 6:9–10 seems to insinuate they, even though they are married, would not make it into the kingdom of God. In essence, it would be a second unforgivable sin besides the blaspheme of the Holy Spirit. Therefore, we need to dig deeper to get to a better understanding as to what this is saying.

Let's look at another passage.

Know ye not, brethren, (for I speak to them that know the law,) how that the law hath dominion over a man as long as he liveth? For the woman which hath an husband is bound by the law to her husband so long as he liveth; but if the husband be dead, she is loosed from the law of her husband. So then if, while her husband liveth, she be married to another man, she shall be called an adulterous: but if her husband be dead, she is free from that law; so that she is no adulterous, though she be married to another man. (Romans 7:1–3)

If you continue to read through verse 7, you will realize this passage is speaking about the new life we have in Christ, which makes us free from the law to be united with Christ by grace through faith.

This passage also seems to say the only thing that allows someone to remarry, without it being adultery, is the death of the spouse.

Let's look at another passage of divorce and remarriage and the allowance of it.

And the woman which hath an husband that believeth not, and if he be pleased to dwell with her, let her not leave him. For the unbelieving husband is sanctified by the wife, and the unbelieving wife is sanctified by the husband: else were your children unclean; but now are they holy. But if the unbelieving depart, let him depart. A brother or a sister is not under bondage in such cases: but God hath called us to peace. For what knowest thou, O wife, whether thou shalt save thy husband? or how knowest thou, O man, whether thou shalt save thy wife. (1 Corinthians 7:13–16)

When an unbelieving spouse leaves, the believing spouse is allowed to let them go. This separation may cause repentance. If the leaving spouse petitions divorce or commits adultery, the believing spouse is not under bondage but free to divorce and remarry.

These passages taken by themselves paint a very stark picture for those who have found themselves remarried or thinking about it. If taken alone, it would seem to relay that if you are divorced and it wasn't because the offending party committed fornication or adultery, then you cannot get remarried. If you are, then this would indicate that you and your new spouse will be guilty of adultery for the rest of your life, and therefore there is no hope for you to enter the kingdom of God. If it is only dissolved by death or abandonment, as the other passages denote, then many are still guilty of adultery and going to hell.

So what do we do then? Never get remarried unless the divorce is by those two stipulations? Do we now divorce the ones we are remarried to because we are committing adultery, or do we stay married—because God is against divorce—but not have intimate relations with our remarried spouse? Understand, if there isn't forgiveness and these people are all going to hell anyway, they might as well stop going to church too. So what do we do?

Realize all doctrine (teaching) comes from scripture, taken in context, compared with other passages of scripture.

This one rule of interpreting correct doctrine is not done by many in the church, including many pastors and church leaders, resulting in much confusion. Some will just not let the Bible get in the way of their beliefs. The treasure of God's Word goes to those who dig for it. So let's continue to dig.

First of all, scripture is very clear, and we can't say that it doesn't give allowances for divorce and remarriage that would not be a sin. So the first thing we have to come to terms with is this: Is divorce that happens without the allowance of scripture sin? Yes.

Let's dig into the passage in Matthew 5:31–32. Here we read that unless adultery has happened, the spouse who remarries and the new spouse will be committing adultery all their lives. Once again, it seems like the unforgivable sin, doesn't it? No wonder so many churches are confused and condemn so many.

Some Key Passages to Help Us Understand This

The key to understanding this is found in the passage with Christ's encounter with the woman at the well.

(Read the whole passage of John 4:1–42.)

I am going to draw some information from some of the verses that will help us understand this.

For thou hast had five husbands; and he whom thou now hast is not thy husband: in that saidst thou truly. (John 4:18)

The woman then left her waterpot, and went her way into the city, and saith to the men, Come, see a man, which told me all things that ever I did: is not this the Christ? (John 4:28–29)

Let's take all these passages and do what we should do with any doctrine or teaching. Let's apply that rule and compare the passages we previously looked at with this one.

Once again, there is the conclusion that many take from the former passages we looked at; based on the passages in Matthew, Romans, and 1 Corinthians, it would seem that if a man or woman is divorced (unless fornication has been committed, total abandonment from an unbeliever, or the death of the spouse) and marries another person, they commit adultery, and it forces the one that marries them to commit adultery for the rest of their life.

This seems, once again, to present a major problem since it plainly states in 1 Corinthians 6:9–10 that such persons will not inherit the kingdom of God. The ones that take such a view have just made divorce and remarriage another unforgivable sin—hell bound with no chance of forgiveness or escape. With this view, there are many in churches wasting their time since there would be no reason to stay. They should all leave, do anything that pleases them, and stop tithing to those churches since they are all doomed to hell anyway. Now, does this really sound like the teaching of Christ? No, it doesn't. This would be the case if there weren't other passages of scriptures to compare.

Divorce and Remarriage Is Not the Unforgivable Sin

The first thing you need to know is divorce and remarriage is not the unforgivable sin. I need to explain what the unforgivable sin is in order to clear any confusion.

Let this solidify the understanding in your heart and mind:

> *Wherefore I say unto you, All manner of sin and blasphemy shall be forgiven unto men: but the blasphemy against the Holy Ghost shall not be forgiven unto men. And whosoever speaketh a word against the Son of man, it shall be forgiven him: but whosoever speaketh against the Holy Ghost, it shall not be forgiven him, neither in this world, neither in the world to come. (Matthew 12:31–32)*

All of Christ's miracles were to point to His power to forgive sins and to save. Those miracles and His words brought the conviction of the Holy Spirit. The Pharisees were saying that Christ's miracles were of Satan, and therefore, they would not allow the Holy Spirit to bring them to conviction so as to receive Christ. Therefore, there will be no forgiveness in this world or in the world to come (before or after death). Are you worried that you have committed this unpardonable sin? Does it concern you greatly? Then that is proof that you haven't. If you had, you wouldn't care. Since you care, the Holy Spirit is ministering to you and working with you. I would encourage you to allow His work in your life and receive Jesus Christ as your Lord and Savior today.

First, understand divorce and remarriage is not the unforgivable sin.

We see this with the woman at the well; she had five husbands! According to some misinterpretation of the other passages, it wouldn't matter if the divorces were her fault or not. She remarried and was in fact currently living with a man; therefore, she could never get to heaven, even if she received Christ.

Someone forgot to tell Jesus Christ this, for it seems He gave her life—eternal life—even though she was divorced and remarried many times. He gave her forgiveness and a restored life. Divorce and remarriage for reasons that aren't biblical allowances is forgivable.

Understand, for this woman at the well, we don't know if she was the offending or offended party of the divorces, but it didn't matter when it came to forgiveness.

I will add one thing that I have heard that is so far off the wall. The thought is this: "Well, she was a sinner, so it could be forgiven, but if she were a believer, then she couldn't have been forgiven." Really? Where is that found in scripture? This doctrine has no place in biblical teaching, for it is absolutely false.

In Matthew, one that has a nonbiblical divorce and remarries - what about that person? Are they doomed to be in sin, even though remarried, and not able to enter the kingdom of God? The answer to that question, as with every habitual sin (since the marriage is an everyday thing), is yes, unless they have both sought heartfelt forgiveness. You don't repent from your new marriage since the new marriage is something God would not want to end in divorce. You do repent from any beliefs or actions that may have contributed to the previous divorce, making the new marriage safe.

This would be the same as with any sin. If you lie one time and don't repent, you are guilty of being a liar for the rest of your life. If you steal and don't repent, you are guilty of being a thief for the rest of your life. However, if you seek true forgiveness, you are forgiven and no longer guilty of being a liar or a thief.

Therefore, there is no doubt that divorce, without biblical grounds, is sin, and it's clear that God hates divorce. It causes damage to them, their witness for Christ, the children, extended family, and the churches they were involved in. Praise God though, there is forgiveness, just as there was for the woman at the well.

Once again, if you are reading this and you haven't been through the divorce yet, stay with your spouse. That is the one God wants you married to.

What then is the answer? Seek Christ's forgiveness with all your heart, and the Lord will forgive you. It's His promise!

> *If we confess our sins, he is faithful and just to forgive us our sins, and to cleanse us from all unrighteousness. (1 John 1:9)*

There is no need to listen to those who want to continue to condemn you. Jesus Christ Himself has set you free.

Remarriage Can Still Be for You

We are going to touch on the subject of someone who says, "Well, to repent, you have to stay unmarried." We need to ask then about the person who has been forgiven and restored. Are they committing adultery if they remarry?

We have touched on the fact that if you are already

remarried, God does not want it to end in divorce. What about the person who is divorced, in right standing with God, but desperately still wants a person in their life?

To understand this, we need to look at the writings of Paul, in the Word of God, on this matter.

First, let's set these verses up. The church in Corinth had written Paul a letter in which they asked about many subjects. One such question was if a person should marry at all. Understand, at this time, Paul was unmarried and dedicated all his effort and attention to the ministry of the Lord. Paul mentions a gift as well, which in this case was celibacy. He had the gift of not desiring or being tempted by sexual sin, even though by the inspiration of the Holy Spirit, he wrote on this subject.

Let's put the following in the context of a divorced person—forgiven but does not have the gift of celibacy, since Christ never gave him/her that gift.

Let's look at verses that will give us guidance in this very important subject.

Now concerning the things whereof ye wrote unto me: It is good for a man not to touch a woman. Nevertheless, to avoid fornication, let every man have his own wife, and let every woman have her own husband. (1 Corinthians 7:1–2)

For I would that all men were even as I myself. But every man hath his proper gift of God, one after this manner, and another after that. I say therefore to the unmarried and widows, It is good for them if they abide even as I. But if they cannot contain, let them marry: for it is better to marry than to burn. (1 Corinthians 7:7–9)

This is very clear. If you are divorced, forgiven, and unmarried, yet you don't have the gift of celibacy, then it is "better to marry than to burn." Paul would have specifically mentioned, "If you are divorced, then this doesn't apply to you," as to avoid any confusion. Paul's chief concern was salvation for all people.

Notice the word "unmarried," which means unmarried. Therefore, when scripture is put together, the meaning is plainly clear. A divorced person who is forgiven, restored, and doesn't have the gift of celibacy can—and, more so, should—get married. In doing so, he or she can avoid fornication and not burn. The only qualification we should always adhere to is the remarried spouse needs to be another born-again, saved person (2 Corinthians 6:14–18).

Does Being Divorced and Remarried Disqualify You from Ministry?

This is one that is a frequent conversation between my lady and me. Between the two of us, we have many years of pastoral and ministry experience. We moved to another area the same month we were married and set out to be available to a church. Long story short, we have been to more than a few churches where we would attend six months to a year, trying to grow closer to the people in the church. One by one, as they found out our story, we were treated differently. The pastors would say we were welcome and they definitely wanted us to use our gifts to serve, but after a while, when one or both of us were not asked to do anything, the message was loud and clear.

In one instance, after going to a church for about a year, I made an appointment with the pastor. I sat down with him and started telling him about our story, and after five minutes, he leaned in and blatantly said, "Listen, I don't care for your years of ministry, but based on what you told me, I will never use you here. You can sit in the chair, but I will never use you."

We were at another church for about a year, and we went to the first fellowship dinner they had since we attended. We sat at round tables, which are normally designed to foster conversations. People were introducing themselves with "How long have you been married?" and "How many kids do you have and what are their ages?" We knew once we answered those questions, they would know we were divorced and remarried. As soon as they understood that, we witnessed something that just shocked us. The person sitting next to my wife turned her chair until the back was facing her, and the person next to me did the same thing. There we were sitting at a round table, realizing that these people we had been in church with for almost a year were shunning us. Understand that my lady and I have been saved for many years, and we could handle the rejection, but what about couples that are new in their faith? How would they be able to handle such rejection from the church?

Going through this as Christians is hard enough, but the rejection in going through it as ministers was rougher still. With that, we are going to look at another aspect of divorce and remarriage. The question is, can a person still be called of God and used in ministry, even if the divorce and remarriage happened after being saved and in ministry?

To understand this, we need to look at the passages that are used by those who don't believe people can be used of God in a divorced and remarried situation.

> *A bishop then must be blameless, the husband of one wife, vigilant, sober, of good behaviour, given to hospitality, apt to teach. (1 Timothy 3:2)*

> *Moreover he must have a good report of them which are without; lest he fall into reproach and the snare of the devil. (1 Timothy 3:7)*

Some try to claim that to be divorced and remarried disqualifies people from being used of the Lord in two ways:

- The husband of one wife—meaning they can't be divorced and remarried.

- Must be blameless—a good report. Evidently, being divorced and remarried is blameful and a bad report.

There are two major flaws with this view. The first flaw with this view is found in the fact that it says, "the husband of one wife," and doesn't mention divorce or remarriage. Every time the Word of God mentions divorce, it mentions divorce or divorce decree/certificate/writing of divorcement. In this passage, the words don't even appear. So what is Paul speaking about then?

He is writing to Timothy, a young pastor sent to Ephesus, a city where pagans lived and where polygamy was practiced. Paul is specifically speaking of polygamy being forbidden.

We also know this from the fact that, if taken at face value, "the husband of one wife" would also mean a widow could not be remarried either, since that verse would make it forbidden. We have no mention of it though; therefore, we know this is applied to polygamy being forbidden.

Also examining the words in verse 2, "blameless," and verse 7, "a good report," some say that means if anything bad could be said about the person, then they don't qualify for ministry. This is flawed on two accounts.

- Every person, before they were saved, had flaws and sins, so they are not blameless and have a bad report.
- Even as believers, we sometimes sin; therefore, in and of ourselves, we aren't blameless. In 1 John 1:8–10, it specifically says we sin, but in Christ there is forgiveness.

Therefore, to keep an unbiblical view of these verses would then disqualify every person, besides Jesus Christ for ministry.

The answer is in how the person is living right now. Are they living for Christ and in His righteousness right now? This is the key question. What is the characteristic of their lives now? Are they striving to become more and more like Jesus Christ? If so, they qualify.

This chapter was deep, I know, yet it needed to be written so that you could understand what scripture plainly teaches when it comes to divorce and remarriage. This had to be clearly revealed so the rest of the book will be understood. You can now read the rest of the book without the question, "Can I even be remarried anyway?" With this question thoroughly answered, you can continue.

Chapter Three

Healing Together—
Mourning and Healing

> To appoint unto them that mourn in Zion, to give unto
> them beauty for ashes, the oil of joy for mourning,
> the garment of praise for the spirit of heaviness;
> that they might be called trees of righteousness, the
> planting of the LORD, that he might be glorified.
> —Isaiah 61:3

There we sat, probably our second or third date, in a very quaint restaurant in an old colonial, remodeled, two-story brick building. It was located right on the riverfront of the Missouri River. She was beautiful, as always, and I could not take my eyes off of her. I held on to every word and sat there in amazement that she was on a date with me.

She had a salad, and I had some sort of sandwich. What I ate exactly, I don't remember, but the lady I was with was etched into my memory, and that date, along with every other, is a memory I will always cherish. Close to the end of the meal, we decided to share a little about the divorces, and that is when I saw the total tenderness of this lady's heart. As she recounted the pain, the tears welled up in her eyes. All I could do was listen and pray, yet, sometimes it is the best thing we can ever do.

That day, I knew and understood a big part of our relationship would be to pray, to love, and to allow ourselves to be used by God for the healing of the other. This healing is a process. This means there will be times you won't do so well, but pray and get right back on the healing process. Doing this will bind the two of you together more than you can imagine.

It All Starts with Your Own Healing

The first step in this process is to realize you must concentrate on your own healing first. This is critically important for your walk with the Lord and for your new marriage. Healing can mend a multitude of wounds from the divorce, and it might need to continue for years into the new marriage, depending on how severe those wounds were.

I remember about a year after my divorce, I was sitting, and my thoughts of my children collided. I saw my kids every day, and then after the divorce, it was every two weeks, and then after a time, it became less. In this one moment, the memories of my kids came flooding in, and the realization of how things would never be the same overwhelmed me. The wave of sadness hit me so hard that I cried for nearly an hour. I prayed through this hour, crying out to God for help, knowing that Jesus Christ was with me through the whole thing. One thing I felt Him say deep in my heart was this: "It will happen again." I understood; I would have other moments that I would mourn and miss the kids as we once were. I will mourn those moments I once had, knowing they will never happen again. Through it all though, I will always know that God will be with me every step of the way.

These wounds can be brought on by different factors of the divorce: guilt from the divorce itself, a complete change in lifestyle, missing the kids, having more responsibility for the kids, financial difficulties, and the ending of other relationships from friends and acquaintances.

The first key to your healing is to admit that you still need healing. It really is okay to mourn. Sometimes sadness hits us, yet in the society we live in, it says we always need to be tough, resilient, and bounce back quickly. Honestly, many just can't, at least not yet. Once again, it's okay to be sad and to mourn. Get this truth deep into your heart and mind; it is not a sin.

Look at some passages that biblically show that to mourn and be sad is not a sin.

> *Then cometh Jesus with them unto a place called Gethsemane, and saith unto the disciples, Sit ye here, while I go and pray yonder. And he took with him Peter and the two sons of Zebedee, and began to be sorrowful and very heavy. Then saith he unto them, My soul is exceeding sorrowful, even unto death: tarry ye here, and watch with me. (Matthew 26:36–38)*

Notice the words, "My soul is exceeding sorrowful, even unto death." Another way of saying this is "I'm so sad it feels like I'm going to die." Realize, Christ felt this way, and He never sinned; so, your feelings and your deep sadness aren't sins either. Anytime sorrow starts to flood your heart, it is good to allow it. It is good to mourn. It is a part of the healing process.

Other people mourned very heavily at times, and the scriptures recount their hearts in the depths of sorrow.

> *I am weary with my groaning; all the night make I my bed to swim; I water my couch with my tears. (Psalm 6:6)*

> *But if ye will not hear it, my soul shall weep in secret places for your pride; and mine eye shall weep sore, and run down with tears, because the LORD'S flock is carried away captive. (Jeremiah 13:17)*

There are different things that will bring each and every one of us to tears. The key is to let yourself have the time of letting the tears roll down your face. Remember, in everything, there is a time. Wise Solomon wrote these words:

A time to weep, and a time to laugh; a time to mourn, and a time to dance. (Ecclesiastes 3:4)

The reason you should allow this is because it is a humbling experience. You may feel the pain and need God's healing—a healing that comes only from God Himself. A healing that touches the mind, heart, and soul.

For the believer in Christ, there are very special promises for God's healing. Realize, when Christ went to the cross, He did it to bring salvation and healing for the whole person: spirit, soul, and body, which touches every aspect of life.

Surely he hath borne our griefs, and carried our sorrows: yet we did esteem him stricken, smitten of God, and afflicted. But he was wounded for our transgressions, he was bruised for our iniquities: the chastisement of our peace was upon him; and with his stripes we are healed. (Isaiah 53:4–5)

That promise is for you in Christ, but He won't do it unless you are drawing close to Him. He will surely hear and heal those who truly call out to Him. The promises keep coming.

The righteous cry, and the LORD heareth, and delivereth them out of all their troubles. The LORD is nigh unto them that are of a broken heart; and saveth such as be of a contrite spirit. (Psalm 34:17–18)

He hears you, delivers you, is close to you, and will save you. Now, this isn't a quick drive-through, microwave-fast prayer. God truly does hear every prayer, no matter how short or long, but when it says, "the righteous cry," these are heartfelt prayers that are truly seeking the Lord out of a broken heart—seeking His help.

Once again, divorce may feel like a living death, but the Lord knows this. He knows how you feel and will lift you up and do something amazing.

> *For thou hast delivered my soul from death, mine eyes from tears, and my feet from falling. I will walk before the LORD in the land of the living. (Psalm 116:8–9)*

It's okay to admit the divorce has wounded you and it feels like death. God will deliver you through it all. There will be a time the tears stop flowing, and the realization will hit you that you are still living and this living is yours to do. Realize there is not only healing through this process, but there will be joy again!

> *They that sow in tears shall reap in joy. (Psalm 126:5)*

This is a joy that only comes from Jesus Christ Himself. It will be a joy that won't make sense. When you start to receive this joy from the Lord, don't let anyone steal it from you.

I remember a season of crying out in tears over and over. One time, I was sitting in the car, and there was a moment the breeze blew through the open windows. It felt like the wind was blowing the sorrow right out of me, and His joy was blowing in. It was a spiritual breeze from God that reminded me of His healing, forgiveness, and comfort.

I was excited about this and shared it with a friend but was surprised to hear the response: "No, brother, I don't believe that was from God; it's too early to feel that."

I was in a place in my life that I was secure in my relationship with God and grounded in His Word, enough to know the truth. The truth that the promises of God have no time frame, and it was real, based on His character as a promise keeper. Even after this joy came, there were still times of sorrow, but there is still healing from God. Concentrating on God's healing would not be complete without the following promise.

Let your conversation (way of living) be without covetousness; and be content with such things as ye have: for he hath said, I will never leave thee, nor forsake thee. (Hebrews 13:5, parentheses added)

In this passage, God is reminding us not to want what we don't have in material possessions but to be content. You can apply this to the situation you find yourself in as well. Your situation may not be good at all, and rest assured, God knows, and He cares very much. The healing, though, comes to you right now, right where you are at. The important thing to realize is God's promise: "I will never leave thee, nor forsake thee."

Let your healing begin!

God Is Healing Your Spouse—Allow Him to Use You

I knew I wanted to marry my lady (the one who had prayed for me) from our first date! It was what we call our "God talk." We went to a lake, sat on a swinging bench, and talked about God: our understanding of Him, the Word of God, our salvation experiences, giftings and callings in ministry. As time went on, we also talked about marriage, not in terms of absolutes, but I was falling in love with her deeply. We spent a lot of time getting to know each other and also took day trips riding our motorcycles. Yeah, she is one fun woman!

The day we got engaged wasn't planned. We were walking by a jewelry store, and I said, "We may as well look so when the time comes, I'll know what you want." She saw the ring, not just a ring but *the* ring. It had white diamonds and chocolate diamonds, with an aquamarine stone, which is her birthstone, set among the diamonds.

She said, "Yeah, that's the one."

The jeweler then said, "It's on sale right now."

I looked at my lady, and she looked at me, and I said, "Well, someone has to be open to a question for that the happen."

My heart burst into joy when she said, "I'm open to that." I asked if she would walk around so that I could look at it more and talk to the jeweler. We met up a little later, and I took her to our favorite Italian restaurant. It was at this moment, through tears, that I asked this precious woman to marry me, and she said, "Yes!"

My time frame for marriage was *now*, but hers was a year or two. I had taken a job two hours away and had moved, so to think of a year or two was killing me. I kept bugging for it to be sooner. She finally said, "Not yet, but when God tells me it's time, I will text you the word *yet*."

It was the time of the year when she normally would have family photos with her kids, so she messaged me to meet her at a special place, to have my kids there for a photo with all of us, as well as to have some engagement photos taken. Now, a little backstory on this location. I took her on another date that had a gazebo very close to the bench where we had our God talk. I played a song on my phone and sang to her while we danced. This special location is where she wanted me to meet her, dressed in the suit she had chosen for me to wear.

The day came when I was to drive up and meet for the photos. I was just so excited to see her, for it had been a couple of weeks. I arrived early, and the only one there was her friend, who was also the photographer. My back was positioned against the parking lot when I got a text containing one word: "yet." I saw that word, and my heart leaped as I remembered what my lady had said. I looked at the photographer, and she was smiling as she looked toward the parking lot. I turned, and the most beautiful sight filled my vision. There she was, all dressed in white, coming over the walk bridge with our kids, other friends, the pastor, and his wife. I was in shock and in tears at the same time. The pastor grabbed me and said, "Today's the day, brother." I was still in shock through most of the ceremony. My lady actually gave me a surprise wedding! I was and am so blessed. She also had planned a surprise honeymoon to Hershey, Pennsylvania—chocolate diamonds and Hershey. Yeah, chocolate was the theme, and my lady is so sweet.

At that moment though, when I saw her coming over the bridge, I cried. This was my dream come true, but it was also like the hand of Christ was upon me saying, "See, my grace is still with you; this is visible proof that I still have plans for you, my son, and those plans include her." What a beautiful day! God had a plan of healing for both of us, and what an amazing beginning!

Understand, from the beginning of your marriage, God wants to use you for each other. Being used of God to help your spouse heal is going to take sacrifice on your part. Just like you are dealing with all the mourning you are going through and all the sorrow, your spouse is going through the same thing—maybe to a greater or lesser degree but the same thing nonetheless.

Here is the biggest key to understanding this aspect, and it's one that you will need the help of Christ through. The key that each of you will have to concentrate on is God healing you as you help the other. It also can't be one-sided from either one of you. You can't demand that you only concentrate on yourself, or demand the other to help you and you not reciprocate it.

In an ideal world, each person would focus on both themselves and the other, but sometimes people focus on just themselves and give no attention to the other. It will seem, at times, like one is taking and taking and not giving. When one is doing this, is all lost? No, of course not. It just takes one to start doing and modeling it correctly, and then over time, the other will see the example and want to help out as well. Over time, the prayer is that both will have a heart for the other; it is why you got married in the first place. In this part though, we are focusing on this: it is not about you but about the other.

There are two verses that will help us understand God's principle of helping others.

> *Let nothing be done through strife or vainglory; but in lowliness of mind let each esteem other better than themselves. Look not every man on his own things, but every man also on the things of others. (Philippians 2:3–4)*

Let's break this down as it pertains to you concentrating on helping and being there for your spouse.

"Let nothing be done through strife or vainglory." In keeping with your marriage and allowing God to use you in healing each other, let this passage guide you as you concentrate on your spouse. Make sure, as much as is in you, to fill the marriage with peace and humility, not strife and vainglory.

I have to be honest and say that I am still working on this myself and may be for the rest of my life. Sometimes, I wanted to help so badly I would try to force healing, but that generated even more strife. As a man, I would look at the process as a machine to get the job done, when in reality, it was fluid like a river. Just as you can't force a river to bend to your will, you can't force the healing process either. It will happen as you cooperate with the river of healing.

Whatever you do, do the best thing for your marriage and create an oasis from the storms of life and the wounds of the past, a place where the presence of Christ is felt. The marriage should be a place where the protective wings of God are realized and felt.

> *Be merciful unto me, O God, be merciful unto me: for my soul trusteth in thee: yea, in the shadow of thy wings will I make my refuge, until these calamities be overpast. (Psalm 57:1)*

"The marriage should be marked with humility." When each spouse lives with lowliness of mind, there is no one taking on the air of superiority in the marriage. At any time in the marriage, if a spouse thinks or acts like they are better than the other, it's a clear mark that humility isn't the driving force. When you are both humble, you can truly complete the third part.

"Treat (esteem) the other better than yourself." When this happens, you won't be self-centered and looking out for number one, for oneself, but your concentration will be looking out for your spouse.

This goes against what our society teaches us. Our society teaches that our own self is all that matters. Many would say, "Just look out for your own healing; your spouse's problems are not yours." Remember "the two shall become one flesh." Now, a problem is both of yours, and that is the way God formed it. Besides, sometimes your best healing is when you allow God to use you to help in someone else's healing. God does miracles with those humble in heart.

But he giveth more grace. Wherefore he saith,
God resisteth the proud, but giveth grace unto
the humble. (James 4:6)

Humble yourselves in the sight of the Lord, and
he shall lift you up. (James 4:10)

If you want more of God's grace, His unmerited favor, then live in humility in your life, including your marriage. Never get to the point of saying, "I don't need you," because we all need one another, especially our spouse. It's God's plan.

"Look not only on your own things." Your marriage doesn't revolve around only you but both of you. Your healing is to be concentrated on first, just not only on yourself. Remember both of you are one in the flesh, so live like it.

"Focus also on the things of others." This means the healing of your spouse; you both need to give encouragement and support to grow closer to Christ and to each other.

The following are practical tips to help you both in being there and helping to heal.

Pray and listen. Be there to pray for and listen to your spouse when they need to talk. Don't force them to open up though. They will talk when they feel safe and comfortable doing so.

Don't take what they say personally; allow freedom. This is a hard one. Don't let what they say be personal and don't get angry with what comes out. Doing so will cause them to not open up. You thought it was hard to wait the first time they opened up; the second time is even worse.

Let me share an example. One time my wife was venting, and words started to come out about not feeling supported and feeling all alone. Well, I took it very personally. Here I was supporting her, loving her, and doing everything I could for her, and she was responding like everything I had done and everything I am meant absolutely nothing to her. Well, I did not respond positively; I showed my utter contempt for what she was saying. Now, looking back on it, I know that was the wrong thing to do. It made her feel unsafe and unprotected to be able to reveal her feelings to me. I showed hurt, and now she felt she must swallow her hurt to try to make me feel better. So, take some good advice and don't take it personally. Do what the Word of God says in the book of James.

> *Wherefore, my beloved brethren, let every man be swift to hear, slow to speak, slow to wrath: For the wrath of man worketh not the righteousness of God. (James 1:19–20)*

Practice the ministry of presence. Don't offer advice unless advice is asked for. In essence, men, don't just try to fix it. Many people, when they are working through something, don't need advice; they just need to know someone cares and is listening.

This helps them process the information they are relaying and allows the Holy Spirit to work out the answers.

A friend loveth at all times, and a brother is born for adversity. (Proverbs 17:17)

We are in essence brothers and sisters in Christ spiritually, so this verse always applies to us.

Ointment and perfume rejoice the heart: so doth the sweetness of a man's friend by hearty counsel. (Proverbs 27:9)

Remember to offer this advice and counsel only when asked. Display great patience with yourself and your spouse; don't rush it. Healing is always in God's timing.

Return, O LORD, deliver my soul: oh save me for thy mercies' sake. (Psalm 6:4)

Love, love, love. Once again, love and put each other first.

This is my commandment, That ye love one another, as I have loved you. Greater love hath no man than this, that a man lay down his life for his friends. (John 15:12–13)

Healing Together

The healing for the married couple needs to be reciprocal, meaning it is to be given by each toward the other. If we apply the previous verses about esteeming our spouses better than ourselves, we will see the marriage fall right into the plan that God has for it right from the beginning. Both spouses need to understand they are both in this together, and God can do a miracle in the marriage.

There is one mind-set that has hurt marriages greatly, and that is the belief that to be a strong individual, you need to live like you don't need anyone else. This may be the world's plan, but it isn't God's plan. Yes, we are individuals, and our lives are individually hidden in Him. It is good to be able to stand in your own faith, whether anyone is standing with you or not. Although this is true, in marriage, God says something very interesting; in marriage, we need each other.

> *And the LORD God said, It is not good that the man should be alone; I will make him an help meet for him. (Genesis 2:18)*

> *Therefore shall a man leave his father and his mother, and shall cleave unto his wife: and they shall be one flesh. (Genesis 2:24)*

Do you see what God is saying here? "It is not good that the man should be alone." The first step in a successful remarriage is to agree with God that it is better to be together than apart.

He then used the words "an help meet for him." What does this mean? It simply means that God designed for the man to have a loving spouse to help him do all the things that God has called and planned for him to be, and he is to be the same for her. In truth, marriage is designed so that both grow closer to Christ, more together than they could apart.

This help for each other is actually a very high calling that each is called to do for the other. It is such a high calling that the same term for "help" (Hebrew *ezer*) is used to describe God Himself.

> *Our soul waiteth for the LORD: he is our help and our shield. (Psalm 33:20)*

> *But I am poor and needy: make haste unto me, O God: thou art my help and my deliverer; O LORD, make no tarrying. (Psalm 70:5)*

Therefore, to be a help for each other is actually a high calling from God Himself. It follows His plan when we help each other out selflessly; it is being more like Christ. Being a Christian means being a follower of Christ or Christlike, and the one we are to show it to more than anyone else in the world is our spouse.

Now that it is clear the two of you are one flesh and are both called to help each other to become everything God has called you to be in Him, let's keep on with this concept.

Two Is Better Than One—Walking Together in Christ

Once again, you are for each other, and God wants to use you through healing and in every other area of life. In marriage, you are one flesh with someone else; therefore, even though you are individuals, you don't have to, nor should you, insist on tackling life's issues on your own any longer. You have a helpmeet there to pray, love, share, and support you through everything. Even if you think the other person doesn't do it well, keep giving them chances over and over again, just like Christ does with you. Practice makes perfect they always say!

> *Two are better than one; because they have a good reward for their labour. For if they fall, the one will lift up his fellow: but woe to him that is alone when he falleth; for he hath not another to help him up. Again, if two lie together, then they have heat: but how can one be warm alone? (Ecclesiastes 4:9–11)*

This passage completely refutes the Lone Ranger mentality and thought stating, "I don't need anyone." God isn't mincing words when He says, "Two are better than one." Realize, isolation is where Satan wants people. When lions hunt, they isolate and attack the one separated from the herd, and Satan is likened to a lion in the same way.

Be sober, be vigilant; because your adversary the devil, as a roaring lion, walketh about, seeking whom he may devour. (1 Peter 5:8)

This is such a concept from God that in Ecclesiastes 4:10b, it says, "But woe to him that is alone when he falleth; for he hath not another to help him up." God truly thinks two are better than one, and that is one of the main reasons He invented marriage.

When a person takes the mind-set they don't need anybody, they can become hardened against people, start disagreeing with God, and think, *One is better than two.* Realize this is a dangerous position to be in, for Satan will have you go down a path that is hard to get back from. The path will look something like this:

- isolation
- a lack of encouragement
- resentment toward those who try hard enough to stay close
- anger toward God
- more isolation from others and God Himself
- an openness to temptations and attacks of the enemy
- hardened toward God and bitter at others because of sin

Through desire a man, having separated himself, seeketh and intermeddleth with all wisdom. (Proverbs 18:1)

In other words, when a person decides they want to isolate themselves, they do not use wisdom properly even though they may know it.

Follow peace with all men, and holiness, without which no man shall see the Lord: Looking diligently lest any man fail of the grace of God;

lest any root of bitterness springing up trouble you, and thereby many be defiled. (Hebrews 12:14–15)

Bitterness can start as something hard to bear, grievous, or full of distress, but it can turn into hostility toward someone if not taken to God. Many marriages fail because unresolved issues create unforgiveness, which can turn into bitterness. This is exacerbated when one isolates themselves.

I need to interject a thought here that even though "two are better than one," the closer that each one is to the Lord, the better the two will be. Just like you need to concentrate on your healing first, the stronger you are, the better you will be together. Although the two of you are one flesh, you still stand before God as individuals. Therefore, as you grow in your marriage, remember growing in Christ for yourself is very important. So understand it is not an either/or thing but a both thing; work on yourself and be there for your spouse as well.

It all starts with focusing on God. It is following the great commandment in your life and is lived out in your marriage. If each individual in each couple is dedicated to this, it does miracles in the healing process.

Jesus said unto him, Thou shalt love the Lord thy God with all thy heart, and with all thy soul, and with all thy mind. This is the first and great commandment. And the second is like unto it, Thou shalt love thy neighbor as thyself. On these two commandments hang all the law and the prophets. (Matthew 22:37-40)

Understand, the important thing to concentrate on is your own healing, loving God with everything you are, but at the same time, give attention to your spouse's healing. This will ensure that Christ will be alive and active in your life and in your marriage. Also, understand something profound that many don't catch in this verse: your spouse is your closest neighbor! Also notice how you are supposed to love them as yourself. Then scripture goes further—to esteem them better than yourself (Philippians 2:3). God's love is unconditional and sacrificial.

This will bring to the marriage a blessing that many miss, but I am praying that you will catch as you read this chapter.

And if one prevail against him, two shall withstand him; and a threefold cord is not quickly broken. (Ecclesiastes 4:12)

This means that God Himself will be intertwined in the marriage, which will make the marriage strong, and it can withstand any attack of Satan, demons, or a person walking in the flesh. The presence of Christ will be greater between you together than if you were alone.

For where two or three are gathered together in my name, there am I in the midst of them. (Matthew 18:20)

Every time you are together, you can be together in His name, and your prayers will be so much stronger and effective than if you were alone.

Again I say unto you, That if two of you shall agree on earth as touching any thing that they shall ask, it shall be done for them of my Father which is in heaven. (Matthew 18:19)

There is no better prayer partner and warrior than your own spouse!

When both spouses realize the principles found in this chapter, you will truly heal together!

Chapter Four

Fighting Ghosts

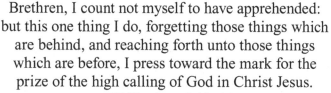

> Brethren, I count not myself to have apprehended:
> but this one thing I do, forgetting those things which
> are behind, and reaching forth unto those things
> which are before, I press toward the mark for the
> prize of the high calling of God in Christ Jesus.
> —Philippians 3:13–14

This chapter will be hard for most, because we want to believe we don't have a problem with it. In this portion of the book, a person will have to humble themselves in the truth, on what they have not overcome and still need to work on. This chapter is called "Fighting Ghosts."

Let me explain this in a simple way and then share some examples.

Fighting ghosts is transferring what a person in a previous relationship has done wrong to the new spouse, based on them saying or doing something similar—whether real or just perceived.

Here's an example that shocked me to the core. My wife and I had an argument, and it was one that we weren't coming to an agreement or understanding on. She stopped and declared that she was going to bed. I was always raised not to go to bed angry, so wanting to give her a hug before she got to bed, I jumped up and ran across the room, down the hall to the bedroom before she could climb in. Well, as I entered the room, she was against the wall with a look of pure fear, and as tears were streaming from her eyes, she yelled at me to "Get away!" I could not understand this reaction for wanting to rush to give her a hug. Through this incident, we discussed it thoroughly. Because of the action from a past relationship, she interpreted my running back to her as something completely contrary to a hug. I was fighting a ghost from her past.

Another example is one I am not proud of. My lady is very beautiful, inside and out, and she is my blessing of grace from Christ. Now, feeling as blessed as I am, there was an increasing fear, from actions in previous relationships that ended because of being cheated on, that this would repeat itself. Well, there were some circumstances that came about that I wrongly interpreted through this lens of the path made by others in my past. I approached her about it, because I needed reassurance that it wasn't happening. Now understand, this was me making her fight the ghosts of my past. I hurt the trust she thought I had in her, and it also hurt because she is a very faithful person, and in this, I was declaring that she wasn't.

With these two examples, it shows that many may have the problem of making their spouses fight ghosts.

The question then is posed: Whether we mean to or not, why do we make our spouses fight these ghosts? Why do we insist on having this in our lives? It sets our spouses up for failure, something they will never win—ever.

The reason we have these ghosts and make our spouses fight them is because we let them still haunt us. Meaning, we never let them die in our hearts and minds and rest in peace. In doing this, we make anyone that moves into our life haunted, fighting these same ghosts. Truly though, we aren't fighting ghosts but our own pains and scars and even demons that still bug and oppress believers.

The answer lies in spiritual warfare over our minds, hearts, and souls.

Work on what you're not over; don't keep something alive that is dead.

These ghosts have power only as long as you give it to them. Most people hate the wounds and damage that someone has done to them, and they don't realize they have let that person's influence stay in their lives—the exact opposite of what they want, sometimes making the new person guilty of the same offense.

Let's take Philippians 3:13–14 again and see how this can apply to our new relationship.

"You have not attained it yet." Understand this truth: if you are making your new love fight this type of battle, then it is proof that you have not attained victory over the past wounds. The step at this point is just to declare to God humbly that you still need His help.

"Forget those things which are behind." This is a challenge and something you are going to truly need the power of God for. The only way to do this is to forgive those who hurt you in the past. You may say, "Oh, I have," but let me make this point. One definition of forgiveness is "the ceasing to punish those for the wrongs they've done to you." If you are making your current spouse fight these ghosts, not only have you not forgiven the past wrongdoer, but you are punishing the new spouse for the sins the past one inflicted on you. You are creating a prison for the new spouse for things they have never done. There must be forgiveness first, even if the other person never asks for it. We need to forgive others just as Christ has forgiven us.

Let's look at how Christ has forgiven us.

As far as the east is from the west, so far hath he removed our transgressions from us. (Psalm 103:12)

And theirs sins and iniquities will I remember no more. (Hebrews 10:17)

This means once God forgives, He doesn't hold it over our heads or continue to punish us for the same sin over and over; it is forgotten. It is also nontransferable in that He doesn't punish someone else for the sins of another.

> *The word of the LORD came unto me again, saying, What mean ye, that ye use this proverb concerning the land of Israel, saying, The fathers have eaten sour grapes, and the children's teeth are set on edge? As I live, saith the Lord GOD, ye shall not have occasion any more to use this proverb in Israel. Behold, all souls are mine; as the soul of the father, so also the soul of the son is mine: the soul that sinneth, it shall die. (Ezekiel 18:1–4)*

Understand, no matter how you look at it, if you are making your new spouse pay for the sins of another, forgiveness has not been done. Now some would say, "Well, we can forgive, but God does not expect us to forgive just like He does." Well, let's see what God Himself says about this.

> *And be ye kind one to another, tenderhearted, forgiving one another, even as God for Christ's sake hath forgiven you. (Ephesians 4:32)*

Notice "even as God" is the same as if it were to say, "just as God."

> *Forbearing one another, and forgiving one another, if any man have a quarrel against any: even as Christ forgave you, so also do ye. (Colossians 3:13)*

Notice, "even as Christ forgave you, so also do ye." Just as He forgives, you forgive. So, yes, God does expect us to forgive just like He does.

If you are a person who plants your feet in the sand, tightens your fists, and says, "I don't care. I'm not going to forgive them and just get over this." The question you need to ask yourself is this: Did you forget how much sin Jesus Christ has forgiven you of?

There is a very strong warning in scripture for you that I would not be able to live with if I didn't include right here. Please read this and reread this to let it sink in.

> *For if ye forgive men their trespasses, your heavenly Father will also forgive you: But if ye forgive not men their trespasses, neither will your Father forgive your trespasses. (Matthew 6:14–15)*

This means exactly what it says. The first time you stopped forgiving someone was the last time God forgave any of your sins, no matter how many times you've asked.

The question you must truly ask yourself is this: Who are you really punishing with your unforgiveness? The answer is truly you but also your new spouse if they are fighting your ghosts.

"Reach forth unto those things which are before." This passage is truly going to bring you freedom and give your spouse freedom from fighting ghosts as well. Reach for the victory that God has placed before you. Once forgiveness has been attained and you shake off the shackles of unforgiveness, then you can step onto the field of victory! Reach instead for those things that are ahead of you. In the concept of marriage, the things that lie ahead are as follows.

Shared growth in Christ. When each spouse concentrates on this for the other, not only is there growth as individuals, there is growth in the Lord as a couple as well. Love grows for God more together than it could ever grow alone. If you are married, God has taken two and has made you one flesh. Your highest goal now, besides growing in Christ individually, is to grow in

Christ as a couple. Everything else comes after. Remember the first institution that God mentioned was marriage. He honors the commitment (Genesis 2:24).

Shared healing. This was covered in the previous chapter, but I want to stress that your healing continues throughout your life. There will be healing from the past, but as a couple, things of adversity will still happen to you and even between you that you will continue to seek Christ's healing for.

Shared freedom. In Christ, there is freedom in living. One thing I want to point out here though is that true freedom can come only one way.

> *And ye shall know the truth, and the truth shall make you free. (John 8:32)*

Be truthful and honest with each other. First, seek out the truth and live for Christ by the Word of God but also cleave to each other in truth. Lies and hidden facts will bind you behind spiritual prison bars. Instead, share and be open so that you give no place for the devil to get a foothold and instead live every day in freedom.

Shared unconditional love. God's love is unconditional.

> *For God so loved the world, that he gave his only begotten Son, that whosoever believeth in him should not perish, but have everlasting life. (John 3:16)*

The word "love" here is the Greek word *agapao*, which means to love unconditionally; to love with contentment.

In a marriage, neither person should feel like they have to earn love based on good performance. This wrong love says, "As long as you do (or do not do) what I want, as long as you don't disagree or cross me, as long as you perform up to my standards, then I will love you." This is not unconditional love and doesn't reflect the goodness and character of God.

Wrong love will put a person in performance bondage, and they will never attain love since, as people, we tend to not always be the best we can be. Unconditional love is full of grace and mercy and loves by choice, by commitment. It says, "I will love you and treat you well no matter what I feel, because my love for you is a choice. I choose to love you."

When two people in a marriage both have this from God and initiate that concept with their spouse, it creates an oasis of love, a place to practically run to in the storms of life. In essence, you both become Jesus with skin on for each other.

Shared purpose. You reach forth with a shared purpose. There is a major twofold purpose for every believer, and that's to love and serve the Lord Jesus with everything you are, and the second is to tell and lead others to Him. Now the specifics and how He does that in your marriage is realized through prayer and study of the Word of God together. Any certain calling, work, education, or goals you individually have will mesh well together, because you two are one flesh, and you will make it work with God's power. You have a shared purpose.

I can do all things through Christ which strengtheneth me. (Philippians 4:13)

You will find protection, comfort, and peace in your shared purpose together. If one of your purposes is bringing turmoil into the marriage and is causing the relationship harm, then that's a good indication that it's not the shared purpose God has called you to.

"Press toward the mark for the prize of the high calling of God in Christ Jesus." There is no better antidote for fighting past ghosts than concentrating on future fulfillments of God's goodness.

There is a high prize in Christ Jesus, and first and foremost, it is salvation. There will be a day, a glorious day in the presence of God Almighty, when you will hear these words:

Enter thou into the joy of thy lord. (Matthew 25:21b)

This will be the prize of the high calling. In the marriage, this prize should be sought out individually and as a couple. Your relationship as a believing husband and wife even models Christ's relationship with the church here on earth. Your marriage itself is a mighty witness and testimony of this relationship (Ephesians 5:21–33).

Marriage is so God honoring that even if one spouse comes to the Lord after marriage and one spouse has still not come to Christ, the marriage is still set aside as good as unto the Lord.

For the unbelieving husband is sanctified by the wife, and the unbelieving wife is sanctified by the husband: else were your children unclean; but now are they holy. (1 Corinthians 7:14)

This isn't saying they have individual salvation by the believing spouse or parent but that the marriage and family are set apart by God as good and legitimate. Therefore, let the marriage be all that it is intended to be, a channel that God uses to help the couple achieve this prize of the high calling in Christ Jesus.

Be Careful to Avoid Triggers

Even though it is each individual's responsibility in a marriage in Christ to gain mastery of making sure you don't cause your spouse to fight your ghosts (seeing your current spouse through the filter of your past), it is also your job to be careful to not pull triggers that bring back the pain of the ghosts in your spouse's past.

For instance, in my wife's past, there was not a lot of affirmation and encouragement for her to make much out of herself. Even with all the obstacles, she persisted through to achieve a bachelor's and two master's degrees and to do very well as a counselor in education and as a Christian speaker and author. For the most part, it was only God and herself working through all the negativity thrown at her saying she couldn't.

Because of this, I have found, by accident, that one of her triggers is anything that says she can't do or be something or anything that resembles a hint that she isn't "good enough." In one argument, I was trying to make a point and sarcastically said, "You should know this as a counselor." Do you know that look when you just crossed a line that you didn't mean to cross? Oh, yeah, I crossed it. It was said sarcastically, and she picked up on the words and tone quickly. This reminded her of her ghosts, and it summoned them back up. When you know the triggers your spouse has, avoid them like a plague!

In every argument, we have all said things we didn't mean, and we sometimes have said things we meant, but we know it wasn't right. Then to compound the problem, when you know a trigger, sometimes, in the heat of the battle, you pull it to inflict hurt on the other. This will continue to put a wedge between you, so instead of seeing each other as an oasis in Christ, you see each other as an enemy, just wanting to inflict harm.

Christ wants you to stop seeing each other as enemies, and instead as husband and wife, as best friends.

These steps will help avoid pulling triggers.

Listen and note the triggers that your spouse has told you about and avoid them. Mine has always been to insinuate I am unintelligent and controlling. I have made great strides to make sure I don't get upset when these are even insinuated, because it says that all my efforts are wasted and I am what I hate the most. That is my trigger. Therefore, listen to the triggers that your spouse shares with you and mentally note the ones you accidentally come across and avoid them at all cost.

Let no corrupt communication proceed out of your mouth. (Ephesians 4:29a)

Let all bitterness, and wrath, and anger, and
clamour, and evil speaking, be put away from
you, with all malice. (Ephesians 4:31)

Realize the most amazing fact: your spouse is the temple of
the Holy Spirit.

What? know ye not that your body is the temple
of the Holy Ghost which is in you, which ye have
of God, and ye are not your own? (1 Corinthians
6:19)

Therefore, know something supremely important: the two of you, as believers, are just as special as the holy of holies in the temple of God. This was the most inner place where the presence of God dwelt and where the high priest would go into once a year (Exodus 26:33–34; 28:29).

When Christ was sacrificed on the cross, the temple veil (which separated the holy of holies from the other parts of the temple) was torn in two from top to bottom. This symbolizes that God Himself has removed anything that separates our access to Him, and now He can live in us (Matthew 27:50–51; Hebrews 6:19).

With this high position of the believer, know that when you start to tear each other down, you are not only hurting each other, you are doing something far worse.

And grieve not the holy Spirit of God, whereby
ye are sealed unto the day of redemption.
(Ephesians 4:30)

When you tear at each other, you are actually grieving the Holy Spirit, for you are trying to tear down a temple of the Holy Spirit. Now, not one of us would picture ourselves going into the temple of God and into the holy of holies of the past and trying to destroy it—for fear that God would strike us dead. Therefore, we should believe the Word of God enough to realize that is what we are doing when we attack each other with the intention to hurt. I encourage you to continue to have a biblical fear of God, knowing that you stand before each other as temples of the Holy Spirit with faces. This next passage speaks of self-destruction and hurting the whole body of Christ, but place this in the context of marriage, and you will understand the gravity of this truth.

> *Know ye not that ye are the temple of God, and that the Spirit of God dwelleth in you? If any man defile the temple of God, him shall God destroy; for the temple of God is holy, which temple ye are. (1 Corinthians 3:16–17)*

Let that sobering thought sink in and allow yourself to see your spouse in that very high and lofty light. The same is true from your spouse to you.

Instead of pulling triggers, speak life!

> *Let no corrupt communication proceed out of your mouth, but that which is good to the use of edifying, that it may minister grace unto the hearers. (Ephesians 4:29)*

> *And be ye kind one to another, tenderhearted, forgiving one another, even as God for Christ's sake hath forgiven you. (Ephesians 4:32)*

So, speak life—words that are filled with love, hope, faith, and perseverance. This becomes easier when you allow God to grow you in the fruit of the Spirit.

> *But the fruit of the Spirit is love, joy, peace, longsuffering, gentleness, goodness, faith,*

meekness, temperance: against such there is
no law. (Galatians 5:22–23)

Notice it says "fruit" of the Spirit and not "fruits," meaning Christ has put the complete fruit in you with all that it entails. Therefore, no one can say, "Well, I have this one but not that one." We have them all when we receive Jesus Christ as our Lord and Savior. Then, through His Spirit, we can live them out more and more.

If you are ever increasing with the fruit of the Spirit and filled with it, then when you are shaken, the only thing that will come out is the fruit. It's similar to shaking a fruit tree; no matter how much you shake it, the only thing that will come off is fruit.

Let your words be used to edify and encourage. Let them be filled with kindness, with a tender tone in heart, and forgive, just like Christ forgave you. This will help you stop making your spouse fight ghosts and will instead build you two through your marriage in Christ.

Chapter Five

Keeping the Peace—Fighting Well

If it be possible, as much as lieth in you,
live peaceably with all men.
—Romans 12:18

The first thing you need to know is this: every successful and healthy marriage has arguments. I know, I know. I just burst someone's bubble again!

Seriously though, a couple that declares they never argue is either lying or there is one who is completely subservient to the other and never lets their voice or opinion be heard. It may seem good to avoid conflict at all cost, but in actuality, it is very unhealthy. This type of marriage may go on for years, but it usually ends with a major conflict that damages everyone involved.

We will take this chapter about keeping the peace and break it down to what a peacemaker is and what happens during arguments. We will also talk about the things God wants us to remember and to practice during disagreements.

Someone may say, "Hold on now. As Christians, we are to never argue. Jesus never got angry, and He never argued. There was never a stern tone in His voice." With this, we really need to break down some scripture to see if this is true.

First, we need to look at a very special promise from Christ Himself.

Blessed are the peacemakers: for they shall be called the children of God. (Matthew 5:9)

That being true, we also need to realize that it doesn't mean there will never be arguments or that an argument shows that you're not a child of God. The same Jesus who made that statement is the same Jesus who used a whip, turned over the money changer's tables, and rebuked them (Matthew 21:12–13; John 2:13–17).

So, unless a person is prepared to say that Jesus Christ is a hypocrite or that He sinned, we need to concede that He was sinless, and even in His anger, He did not sin (Matthew 5:22; Mark 3:5). Therefore, there needs to be a greater understanding of what a peacemaker is.

One thing you need to do is to get it out of your mind that if you ever raise your voice, take a tone, or get angry, it makes you a horrible person and an unbeliever; otherwise, once again, Jesus has some big issues that He needs to explain. The truth is, it is what you do and say in that anger that may result in sin.

What does Christ mean by being a peacemaker?

To answer that question, we need to answer a different question. When would we ever need peacemakers? We need peacemakers when peace is broken and disagreements have taken place.

I don't know if you realize this, but we are people, imperfect people, so there are going to be disagreements. If you have ever been to an annual church business meeting, you know that disagreements happen in the church as well as in the home. How these disagreements are handled by you will reveal if you are a peacemaker or not.

Why do we have disagreements in the first place? Well, the reason we have disagreements is there are two people who may be looking at the same issue from two different perspectives.

These different perspectives happen a lot because a lack of communication keeps them from getting on the same page.

For an example, it is like two people looking at the painted number six on the pavement, one is standing on one side and declares it is the number six, and the other is standing on the other and declares it is the number nine. Both are right from their perspectives, but it takes communication for them both to look at the context and see the numbers that may be painted in sequence next to it to figure it out. It takes communication and a willingness to work through it.

We need to answer this question: Does God want us to be in complete unity? Yes, and this is a good thing.

> *Fulfil ye my joy, that ye be likeminded, having the same love, being of one accord, of one mind. (Philippians 2:2)*

So the answer again is yes, God does expect unity from His children, but that can only be done through complete communication. Once communication breaks down, more and more disagreements will happen because they are turning the pages at different times.

Disagreements will happen, and this is why we have the passage in Romans that gives very practical advice.

> *If it be possible, as much as lieth in you, live peaceably with all men. (Romans 12:18)*

Do you see that phrase, "If it be possible, as much as lieth in you"? This means do as much as you can to continue in peace, and when it is broken, do everything you can to restore that peace.

We shouldn't get too upset when we disagree sometimes, because it can help us learn to lean on God as we wait to get on the same page again. It helps us learn the character of Christ and become more and more like Him.

So what are the characteristics of a peacemaker?

Peacemakers Are Holy

That means that they are set apart from the world and dedicated to Jesus Christ.

> *Follow peace with all men, and holiness, without which no man shall see the Lord. (Hebrews 12:14)*

Understand that the closer you are to Christ, the more holy you become, so as you become more holy, you will be more like the Prince of Peace, Jesus Christ Himself.

The world's ways are always to have conflict, rage, and war. Do not let the world creep into you; it will bring it into the marriage. Holiness and peace go hand in hand, so if there is a lot of conflict going on, check your life first. First, see if there is anything inside of you that is offensive to God, sinful, or worldly. Be honest with yourself, for the first one you need peace with is the Lord Jesus.

> *Search me, O God, and know my heart: try me, and know my thoughts: And see if there be any wicked way in me, and lead me in the way everlasting. (Psalm 139:23–24)*

Understand there must be true eternal peace in your heart and soul for there to be the ability to be a peacemaker in Christ with your spouse. A good place to start is forgiveness (refer back to the chapter "Fighting Ghosts").

Peacemakers Are Loving

We start with holiness first, for that begins when our relationship with God begins, but then we grow in His love. God is love, and in our relationship with Him, we love others, and the first one in line is our spouse.

Beloved, let us love one another: for love is of God; and every one that loveth is born of God, and knoweth God. He that loveth not knoweth not God; for God is love. (1 John 4:7–8)

So many people say they love God, but in the midst of conflict and disagreement, they display almost pure hatred and disdain for each other in word and actions, or one or both ignores the other's existence for days.

Be loving just like Jesus Christ, who came and laid down His life to bring us peace because of His love for us. In fact, He could have said, "Nope, I am not lowering myself to prove that I love them." Instead, in His love, He gave us His all.

But God commendeth his love toward us, in that, while we were yet sinners, Christ died for us. (Romans 5:8)

Let us love sacrificially like Christ does, especially toward our spouses.

Peacemakers Are Longsuffering

Some translations use the word patience for longsuffering, but it really doesn't do it justice like longsuffering, because it means to "suffer long."

When you go through a time of fighting, you want the other spouse to be fixed, and you think they should be fixed immediately. Sometimes we may think, *They should be able to see where they are wrong. God is big enough to change them— and immediately—if they really want it.* Realize that they are thinking the same thing about you.

Peacemakers who are longsuffering understand that the processes of understanding each other is just that—a process.

I know an old retired minister who shared his life and ministry with his wife for more than sixty years. One day, in a men's ministry meeting, some guys asked him what the secret was for a long, successful marriage. His answer was simple. "Love her deeply, communicate often, and be longsuffering." (He winked at the word longsuffering).

He went on to tell us that He is still discovering his wife, still learning about her, and still—yes—having arguments. Through this, they continue to learn about each other and fall more in love every single day.

Do you see the magnitude of this? A marriage of more than sixty years, and they still have arguments. They're still learning about each other and growing closer. This takes longsuffering; it is a commitment for life no matter what.

Many people, nowadays, believe that having an argument is proof that you shouldn't be together and insinuate that in every argument. There may not be an argument for days, weeks, or even months, but the first sign of a disagreement, one mentions that it was a mistake to get married. Realize there is no safety fostered here. There is no long-term commitment displayed. This only makes the other spouse walk on pins and needles since at the slightest argument, they are going to be told that they shouldn't be together. There will be more on this later, but for now, if you find yourself saying this in every argument with your spouse, God is strongly encouraging you to lose it from you list of digs to use in an argument.

Allow each other the process to learn and to grow. Being a peacemaker means knowing that disagreements will happen and that we need to learn to love through arguments and treat them as opportunities to draw closer to each other instead of tearing each other apart; that is the true work of a peacemaker. This takes being longsuffering, which God has already given you.

But the fruit of the Spirit is love, joy, peace, longsuffering. (Galatians 5:22a)

No matter what age, some believe that after a great wedding, everything will be blissful. In fact, for most, the beginning of the marriage can be the roughest part, because you are learning each other. We will go through this more in a later chapter. The important thing to remember is that both spouses in a marriage need to be longsuffering and patient. Keep up with the marriage and actively pursue each other's heart for the rest of your lives. It will get better and better; it's a promise from God!

> *Better is the end of a thing than the beginning thereof: and the patient in spirit is better than the proud in spirit. (Ecclesiastes 7:8)*

It is going to get better and better! This verse provides a reminder of the next point.

Peacemakers Are Humble

In a marriage where two become one flesh (Genesis 2:24), there is truly no room for pride. Pride at its core is selfish and declares, "I'm first!" Let's say there is an argument, and it's a bad one. One may even say these words, "I'm not going to let you into my life anymore!" After that, they will make sure no forgiveness is accomplished the way Christ wants, and then they will allow the bitterness to keep them from that person so they don't get hurt again. Realize, even though you think you are protecting yourself, it is also pride to the greatest extent, for it says, in actuality, "What I'm doing is wrong, but in my pride, I said what I wanted to say, and now I have to keep my word. If I let you in, then I have to go against my word, and I won't do that!"

Realize you are setting yourself up higher than God. When dealing with the evil city of Nineveh, God pronounced a judgment on them:

> *Arise, go to Nineveh, that great city, and cry against it; for their wickedness is come up before me. (Jonah 1:2)*

And Jonah began to enter into the city a day's journey, and he cried, and said, Yet forty days, and Nineveh shall be overthrown. (Jonah 3:4)

And God saw their works, that they turned from their evil way; and God repented of the evil, that he had said that he would do unto them; and he did it not. (Jonah 3:10)

Understand what happened. God repented. He gave His word, but because the people changed, He changed His mind and did not destroy the city.

Marriage is the place where each spouse learns and then displays humility, primarily toward each other. It is a committed partnership where neither one declares, "It's my way only." There is going to be a chapter later that goes into this concept in depth, but the point here is the attitude must be one of true humility that has, at its core, to esteem and treat the other spouse better than oneself.

Humility, for any person, shows the attitude of Jesus Christ Himself, and this is what we want to display to each other in our marriage. Humility continues the grace and work of God in our lives individually, which brings the grace of God into our marriage as well. This attitude of humility will foster a safe haven of love and create a marriage where each can feel the presence of Christ from the other.

But he giveth more grace. Wherefore he saith, God resisteth the proud, but giveth grace unto the humble. (James 4:6)

Humble yourselves in the sight of the Lord, and he shall lift you up. (James 4:10)

Therefore, in your individual life, if you are governed by pride, then you are being resisted by God. He is not allowing some things in your life to come to fruition (resisting you) in order to wake you up to the problem of pride. The detrimental thing is that this also carries over into the marriage since you are one flesh. This is even worse if both spouses have a problem with pride. If, on the other hand, humility reigns in your lives, then God does something amazing. According to His Word, He gives more grace, which is unmerited favor, giving us what we don't deserve, and He lifts us up.

The characteristic of humility in each spouse individually will bring that same characteristic into the marriage and will foster a safe haven of love, creating a marriage where each can feel the presence of Christ from the other.

Peacemakers Strive for Peace—Positive Talk

Be ye angry, and sin not: let not the sun go down upon your wrath: Neither give place to the devil. (Ephesians 4:26)

Be Angry and Sin Not

There is an old saying that we have all heard as children that we can apply here; "If you can't say something nice, don't say anything at all." This is so true and applies perfectly to a marriage.

This verse shows that one can be angry, and it is not a sin. It is what one does in that anger that can be the sin. In an argument, it usually comes out in the words spoken. We have all been in an argument where we hear words come out and we think, *Oh no. I can't believe I just said that!* It's out, and you can't take it back.

In remembering that peacemakers are humble, the right course of action is to ask forgiveness for the words that you said, and if spoken to you, the response is to forgive. If pride governs your actions, the words come out, but the actions are as follows.

If you said the words: "So what? I said it! I meant it and will not feel bad I said it! I will not apologize! That's for a weak person, and I'm not weak!"

If the words are said to you: "I don't care if they apologize. I will not forgive them. They said it, and therefore they meant it and will pay for it!"

First, if you have said things that wounded your spouse, don't just blanket apologize. Be specific for what you are sorry for. Those words can cut very deep, and your spouse needs to know that you regret saying the words and that you truly don't feel that way. Remember—don't let pride stop you from seeking forgiveness because "you always mean what you say." Even if you did, you know it wasn't right; seek forgiveness still.

With God's help, you can be angry and not sin. The tongue can cause much damage. Let's look at how God looks at this double speech from our mouths.

> *But the tongue can no man tame; it is an unruly evil, full of deadly poison. Therewith bless we God, even the Father; and therewith curse we men, which are made after the similitude of God. Out of the same mouth proceedeth blessing and cursing. My brethren, these things ought not so to be. (James 3:8–10)*

These verses demonstrate how God views us when we lift up our spouse one moment and tear them down the next. This should not be! Instead, we should be blessing them every time we speak. Now, with that statement, I heard in my spirit someone say, "Then I can't speak at all, because I have nothing good to say." Then you truly need to pray that God touches your heart. Your heart is what truly needs to be worked on, and God can do it.

A good man out of the good treasure of his heart bringeth forth that which is good; and an evil man out of the evil treasure of his heart bringeth forth that which is evil: for of the abundance of the heart his mouth speaketh. (Luke 6:45)

So when you are in the heat of an argument, at any time, let these next verses come to your mind and heart and allow it to guide you.

Wherefore, my beloved brethren, let every man be swift to hear, slow to speak, slow to wrath: For the wrath of man worketh not the righteousness of God. (James 1:19–20)

Hear the issue! There is an old saying about this verse: God wants us to listen twice as much as we speak, since He gave us two ears and one mouth. It may seem comical, but really, it's good practical truth.

"Be swift to hear." Be eager and ready to really listen. Listen to the words even through the tone. Many don't listen to the words because they can't get past the tone or the emotions from which they are said. They can't get past the facial expressions, gestures, and sometimes even mocking. It takes the grace of God to do this, but don't get sidetracked by thinking in an argument that no one will get loud or yell or have an unkind tone, especially if it has already escalated. But it only takes one to start to defuse the whole thing, by really cutting through and listening to the words spoken. Process the words themselves and try not to be offended by the delivery of them.

Instead, listen. Truly listen. Be quick to hear. In fact, approach every disagreement with the desire to listen more than you want to "say your peace," because peace is sometimes not your motivation.

"Be slow to speak." This is one rule here that I can't

emphasize enough. Truly listen, and while they are speaking, don't be trying to figure out your response.

My lady and I have been in arguments when the response was said to a statement that was never really said by the other. The problem was the response didn't even match what was said by the other. Why was that? The reason is that we were thinking of our response; therefore, we weren't listening to what was being said, so we missed it altogether, and this made the argument escalate to an unproductive bunch of noise. So be slow to speak.

Let me add a direction for this thought. This is going to be a hard one that you will need the power of God to accomplish. You also will not want to do this, because it really takes swallowing your right to be right and let things go.

Here is a great rule to establish for yourself. Underline this, highlight this, and remember this. When you speak with your spouse, only speak what is positive or neutral, but if it may be taken negatively, then give this to God in prayer and let Him take care of it.

Stick to this no matter how hard. If only one person in the argument initiates this, then the argument not only deescalates, but it empties it of the fuel. These verses can help in this situation.

Do all things without murmurings and disputings.
(Philippians 2:14)

Murmuring and disputing include saying negative things under the breath or just low enough that they can't completely hear. Remember they are the temple of the Holy Spirit, just like you.

Realize that in bad arguments, both people lose. The only way for both to win is to not get into heated arguments to begin with. The goal is to be able to work through disagreements without seeking the world's way of fighting. When we fight, we are placing ourselves as number one and fighting for our own way. Instead, putting everything in the Lord's hands and following His way will bring healing.

> *For all seek their own, not the things which are Jesus Christ's. (Philippians 2:21)*

God gives you the strength to seek that which is of Jesus Christ.

> *For it is God which worketh in you both to will and to do of his good pleasure. (Philippians 2:13)*

"Slow to wrath." Doing this will keep the calm, which will cause you to be slow to anger—for the anger of humans gets in the way of God's righteousness. One great practical direction that the Bible gives is this: "Do not let the sun go down on your wrath."

Why does God give this command to us? The reason is very important and penetrating.

Before we go into why, we need to realize that this is a command for the individual, and within the context of marriage, it applies to both partners. This means, if an argument has transpired, there needs to be closure; the reconciliation needs to be accomplished before you go to sleep. Too many couples just get to the point that the argument ends, but there is no discussion, no making it right, and then they go to bed with minds on the conflict and wounds in the heart.

Sometimes, someone says they aren't mad and goes to bed, leaving the other one with unresolved feelings. Even if this is not always the case, the one who goes to bed could be sending the message that, after giving so much energy to help escalate the argument, now they don't think the relationship is important enough to spend any energy in helping resolve the issue. Once again, even though this may not always be the complete truth, it can send that message.

This just sweeps things under the rug, only to be tripped on another day. Rehashing the points of the argument without constructively coming to a good spot goes against what God is commanding.

Understand that when you let the sun go down on your wrath, it leads to playing the issue over and over and even dreaming about and stressing over the unresolved issue all night. God is very clear about this and what happens; it gives a place to the devil.

So when you take this command for granted and don't obey the Lord's instruction, you open up a place for the devil to start his work. What is the work that the devil does when this happens over and over? He creates bitterness.

Just a few verses down from the verse saying to not let the sun go down on your wrath, we have these verses:

> And grieve not the holy Spirit of God, whereby ye are sealed unto the day of redemption. Let all bitterness, and wrath, and anger, and clamour, and evil speaking, be put away from you, with all malice. (Ephesians 4:30–31)

Since we are temples of the Holy Spirit, it makes no sense to be bitter at a temple of the Holy Spirit. Therefore, let's examine bitterness and what it does.

What is bitterness? Bitterness is intense antagonism or hostility toward someone—hard to bear, grievous, and distressful. Simply put, if you think of your spouse and it doesn't bring a pleasant thought or it makes you grievous, you are bitter toward them. When one allows things to be unresolved and fester, bitterness comes, and many times it sets in.

> Looking diligently lest any man fail of the grace of God; lest any root of bitterness springing up trouble you, and thereby many be defiled. (Hebrews 12:15)

Now the Greek really brings this to light; "bitterness" is *pikria*, acridity (sharp and stinging) as a poison—exceedingly caustic (capable of burning, corroding, or destroying living tissue).

Do you catch the fact that bitterness is not a good thing and why it will trouble you? If not taken care of, it will defile you. Bitterness happens when we depart from living in and showing the grace of God. So how do you fight the root of bitterness? Always be mindful of the magnitude of the grace of God shown to you, which is His unmerited favor, giving you what you don't deserve.

Grace is from the heart of Christ.

Grace genuinely smiles at the person showing the attitude.

Grace forgives even when not asked.

Grace shows mercy when they don't deserve it.

Grace says, "Forgive them, for they know not what they do."

Understand that grace, when lived and displayed, will dig down and be the root that fills the ground of your life, and the root of bitterness will not find a place.

One last point on fighting well.

Keep It to the Situation

"Well, maybe we shouldn't even be together!" Maybe words like that have been spoken by one or both of you. Maybe these words were the end words spoken that started from something as simple as deciding what to watch for entertainment—comedy or drama. Many couples take an issue that they are discussing and escalate it to this degree. It's like steps of engagement.

First step—the issue at hand. Stay on the issue and keep it on target. Don't go to the next step.

Second step—generalities. Sometimes people shift to generalities that are not even on the subject at hand. Avoid statements such as "You never!" or "You always!" It is very degrading because it takes the large strides that someone has taken and flushes them down the proverbial toilet as soon as there is a disagreement. Never let the conversation go to the next step.

Third step—relationship. This is the step where bitterness is displayed and fostered. This step is the worst step to get to, and many jump to this step at the slightest provocation. A disagreement in finances leads to "We shouldn't be married." A disagreement in how to discipline the kids leads to "We should have never gotten married." A disagreement in anything that results in attacking the relationship is going to create an ultimate fear of ever having a disagreement, and it will force one to be subservient in the relationship, just to never hear these relational fatalistic words.

One good visual, practical thing to do is to decide on an object; it could be a pillow, a piece of cloth, or something else that is called "the issue object."

When an issue ensues, and a disagreement happens, if at least one party feels that it may start an argument, they should stop and pray together for God's guidance, mercy, grace, and wisdom (you won't believe how many issues die right here). Then hold the issue object. Declare the issue object as the issue and throw it from the both of you onto the floor. Now you have visually separated the issue from the relationship of the two of you. You will now discuss that issue and only that issue. This will help prevent it from ever going to the second step, generalities, and the third step, relationship. It keeps it to the issue at hand.

My prayer is that you will take the concepts from this chapter, based on the Word of God, and let Christ's love, grace, and mercy help you both to keep the peace. Let the peace of God flourish in your marriage!

Chapter Six

Compromise Is Not a Bad Word

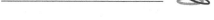

It's All about Teamwork

> This is my commandment, That ye love one another,
> as I have loved you. Greater love hath no man than
> this, that a man lay down his life for his friends.
> —John 15:12–13

Have you ever done or said something that makes your spouse
so upset, and you have no idea why? Yep, we have all been there
and done that! Here's an example. My wife had just steamed
some broccoli and cauliflower in a bowl. I walked by and said,
"Oh nice, yum," and picked one up with my fingers and popped
it into my mouth. As I savored the taste of the steamed veggie,
I noticed my wife staring at me with the most disgusted face I
had seen from her. When I asked why she was looking at me
like that, I thought I had crossed another line. Oh my! I did two
major no-nos. The first thing was I touched the food with my
fingers. The second was that I had to ask why it disgusted her.

Understand, I wasn't brought up as properly as she was, so
it wasn't a big deal to even try something off someone's plate,
just as long as you didn't take it off the fork as it was on the
way to the mouth! My lady, though, was quite different, so I
made her another bowl. I compromised my position and don't

do that anymore. I will go for a chip out of a bag or a nut out of the jar only if I ask her first. This is called compromise; I compromised and adjusted the way I did things, and she compromised by allowing certain foods when I ask.

So what does compromise mean? It is a settlement of differences by mutual concession; it's a give and take.

Compromise Is a Part of Life

Now, what I am about to share is information and conclusions I have pulled from the Word of God and also what I learned from being a pastor and giving spiritual guidance and premarital and marital instruction to couples.

I was always intrigued by the culture that said marriages would last longer if people would wait until later in life to get married. Well, what I was observing through many couples was that it went against common sense. Also, it depends on how long they lived at home or on their own. Here is the difference. If you look back over the last few generations, many of our grandparents and great-grandparents married right out of high school or during or right after college. They were still accustomed to working together and compromising with others, whether they were parents, siblings, or dorm mates. When marriage happened, they were still accustomed to working with others and compromising with others to live well together.

If, on the other hand, people live on their own for a while, they choose to do their own thing—what they want, with whom they want, and when they want. They seem to have set all their preferences for life. Then they get married, and suddenly there are instances where they must compromise and work together. If either one or both spouses don't budge but instead plant their feet and demand that they will not change, the relationship is headed for failure. With Christ's help though, they can have an amazing marriage.

Let's look at two parts of being a team with your spouse.

Love Your Spouse Dearly and Always Remember You're a Team

Why did I use "love your spouse" for this section? Unless love is your underlying motivation, any compromise will be met with resentment. Understand, love for your spouse will get you to want to do things that please them. You will do and not do things, break habits and customs because your desire and love for your spouse is your motivation. There is no greater love than to lay down your life for your friends. If you love your spouse enough to lay down your life, then you will find it easy to love them enough to change a preference.

Love is the greatest part of this. Remember a husband has a very high calling for the wife and the wife has a high calling for the husband.

Husbands

At this point, I am going to speak toward the men. Both are under this command, and it is missed by many. Let's dig into these two verses.

> *Submitting yourselves one to another in the fear of God. (Ephesians 5:21)*

> *Husbands, love your wives, even as Christ also loved the church, and gave himself for it. (Ephesians 5:25)*

Remember we are to love and treat our wives as Christ loves and treats the church. He did it so much that He humbled Himself, came to live as a man, and sacrificed His very life for the church. Men, not only should you be willing to sacrifice and die for your wife, but you should be willing to sacrifice your desires, preferences, and habits for your wife. She is your first called person for you to love and minister to.

I have known relationships where the husbands put ministry,

careers, other family members, children, and even a hobby before their wives, and this is clearly unbiblical. The wife is left feeling unneeded, devalued, and completely unwanted. Understand, Christ would never treat His bride, the church, like that, and we are not to treat our wives like that either. Instead, we should be willing to lay everything down so that the wife can be everything God has designed her to be.

> *That he might present it to himself a glorious church, not having spot, or wrinkle, or any such thing; but that it should be holy and without blemish. (Ephesians 5:27)*

Your goal should be that your wife is better and draws closer to Christ with you in her life, more than without you.

Wives

Now, wives, a word to you. This passage has been abused, but it is in the Word of God and God's direction to you, so do not get your black highlighter out and start marking (yeah, you get it), because it has been taught wrongly or you have interpreted it wrongly.

In the order that God has established, realize that Christ never asks you to be or do something that He Himself doesn't fully know. Look at the Godhead; it is one God made up of three persons—God the Father, God the Son (Jesus Christ), and God the Holy Spirit. Though each are equal with each other in nature, divinity, power, and character, we see a difference in office and work. The Son submits to the will of the Father, and the Holy Spirit submits and points to the Son.

In our Christian walk as husbands and wives, first realize that we are equal in the Lord in nature as believers.

> *There is neither Jew nor Greek, there is neither bond nor free, there is neither male nor female: for ye are all one in Christ Jesus. (Galatians 3:28)*

Therefore, let this point be abundantly clear: submission does not refer to being less than or not equal to the husband but an acknowledgment of the difference in office and work in the family; it a choice to fall under the leadership and protection of the husband.

Realize, the husband is called to give his life, wants, and desires and to submit to your needs, to help you be all you can be under his protection and leadership in the Lord.

Someone may be asking, "But what happens when I don't agree with a decision he has made? Do I have to submit then?" To this point, there is only one reason you are to not submit to your husband. Let's look at this verse clearly and see what it says.

> *Wives, submit yourselves unto your own husbands, as unto the Lord. (Ephesians 5:22)*

Let us first clear the air of false teaching. Women are *not* supposed to submit to every man; that is not biblical. A wife is to submit to her *own* husband. She is to only come under the leadership and protection of her own husband and not another man. The only exception would be to church leadership when it comes to spiritual and church issues (Hebrews 13:17).

The next part of the verse we are going to concentrate on is this: you are to submit as unto the Lord. There are two parts I want to bring up about this part of the verse.

As unto the Lord. Christ will never ask you to do or not do something that would go against His Word—ever!

A bold example was a man who tried to command his wife to watch pornography with him to spice up the marriage; this is not "as unto the Lord," so she is to *not* be submissive to this direction at all. A specific instance when he asks you to disobey God's Word is not to be obeyed.

As unto the Lord. Just as you would submit to Christ, submit the same way to the husband's leadership and guidance.

Remember that God placed your husband to protect you and

to provide leadership. Just like Christ—even though equal with the Father, He never once revolted and said to the Father, "No, I am equal with you and don't have to submit to your leadership!" That would be pride, but Christ was completely obedient, even though He may have wanted something else.

> *And he went a little further, and fell on his face, and prayed, saying, O my Father, if it be possible, let this cup pass from me: nevertheless not as I will, but as thou wilt. (Matthew 26:39)*

The cup represented the sins of the world—the moment of feeling the full weight of sin for everyone who has sinned, past, present, and future and the wrath, guilt, and harm from the effects of that sin. With it came the climax on the cross.

> *And about the ninth hour Jesus cried with a loud voice, saying, Eli, Eli, lama sabachthani? that is to say, My God, my God, why hast thou forsaken me? (Matthew 27:46)*

Understand this was a very painful moment for Christ. Even going into the garden of Gethsemane to pray, Jesus said some words to indicate the uttermost sadness for this submission task He was about to undergo to the will of God the Father.

> *Then saith he unto them, My soul is exceeding sorrowful, even unto death: tarry ye here, and watch with me. (Matthew 26:38)*

In other words, He was so sad that He felt like He would die.

So what does this show us about submitting and how Christ submitted? You don't submit only when you want to or when it is guaranteed to bring pleasant results. Christ submitted to the will of the Father even when, in the moment, He prayed that it would pass from Him.

Now, a wife may say here, "Well, Christ knew that God the Father wouldn't make any mistakes, so what do I do when I know or feel that he is about to make a mistake?" This poses a good question when it comes to compromising with each other. The first thing that should be happening once again is found in Ephesians.

> *Submitting yourselves one to another in the fear of God. (Ephesians 5:21)*

There should be a submitting of one to another, sharing ideas and concerns and coming to a consensus on decisions and things of importance. Here though is the rub. What happens when there is a decision to be made yet there are two separate opinions as to what to do?

The answer to that question is easy: What would Jesus Christ do? He submitted to the will of the Father. In these cases, as a wife, you need to look at some facts and ask some questions toward the decision. Is it biblical? Does it line up with holy scripture? If it is and does, and you are just kicking against it because you see it as a wrong decision, then take Christ's example and follow.

Therefore, if it doesn't go against the Word of God but you just don't like the decision, submit to the leadership decision of your husband. Why in the world would you do this? Going back to a previous statement, the goal of the Christian marriage is that each one would draw closer to Christ, together more than if you were apart. What happens when the decision ends up being wrong and may even cause some harm or trial to him or both of you? Now to this, let's look at this passage in James.

> *My brethren, count it all joy when ye fall into divers temptations; Knowing this, that the trying of your faith worketh patience. But let patience have her perfect work, that ye may be perfect and entire, wanting nothing. (James 1:2–4)*

God uses the good, the bad, and the ugly to make you who you are, to grow you and to perfect and mature you. We have another passage.

And we know that all things work together for good to them that love God, to them who are the called according to his purpose. (Romans 8:28)

Do you truly believe this verse—I mean really believe it? If you answered in the affirmative, good!

Therefore, do you think that even with a wrong decision (as long as it isn't unbiblical), and the positive result doesn't happen or even a negative result ensues – good can still happen? Do you think God can and will use it for his good to work patience, to make him and you perfect and entire, wanting nothing? I firmly believe so.

Most make decisions so that no matter what happens, they can control the outcome and not have to be in a place that they have to trust God. Realize that this doesn't increase your faith, but stretching your trust in God is what builds lasting faith.

Understand, through it all, that your husband will be built and grow in his faith, and you will be built in yours as well. You will also be rewarded simply by obeying the Word of God in this.

Let me share a good illustration on submitting and the proper understanding of it. Let's pretend that you come home late at night and that as you get out of your car and walk toward your door you notice a big man standing in your path. You panic, and your heart races as you turn to run the other way. As you run down the sidewalk, you notice a police car pull onto your street, with the guy following close behind. The officer sees you, stops, and gets out of the car, at which you immediately get behind him, maybe even clutching his arm. This is you biblically submitting to his protection and leadership. You trust that he has the wisdom to lead and guide you, just like you trust God has prepared your husband to do the same.

Even if the officer makes a decision you don't want to submit to, you do. Maybe you think he should have grabbed the shotgun instead of the pistol or that both of you should just drive away really fast. In that moment that you don't agree, do you throw a tantrum, declare he made a wrong decision, and march away from him to fight the attacker on your own? No! Even though you may disagree with his tactics, you choose to submit. Realize in this scenario that the officer is putting himself in harm's way and is willing to die to protect you if need be. It is easy in this scenario to see the proper biblical example for both the husband and the wife.

Both Husbands and Wives

This brings us to one last point on this part, and we need to understand this very clearly.

> *Nevertheless let every one of you in particular*
> *so love his wife even as himself; and the wife*
> *see that she reverence (respects) her husband.*
> *(Ephesians 5:33, parentheses added)*

Husband, you are to compromise in such a way that you submit to your wife's needs and you love her even as yourself. If it isn't unbiblical and you need to give up a preference to meet her need, you give it up.

Just like the police officer in the scenario would do anything to protect the woman, men, you are on the front line of defense. God has placed you to lead and protect but also to nurture your wife to be all she can be in the Lord.

We are living in a day that the enemy of our souls is attacking in almost every way, especially spiritually.

> *For we wrestle not against flesh and blood, but*
> *against principalities, against powers, against*
> *the rulers of the darkness of this world, against*
> *spiritual wickedness in high places. Wherefore*

take unto you the whole armour of God, that ye may be able to withstand in the evil day, and having done all, to stand. (Ephesians 6:12–13)

This means, men, not only for yourself but also for your wives, you need to be praying, studying the Word of God, and living in the Lord to fight against the enemy that comes against you and your marriage. Love her with the same love of Christ!

Finally, my brethren, be strong in the Lord, and in the power of his might. Put on the whole armour of God, that ye may be able to stand against the wiles of the devil. (Ephesians 6:10–11)

Wives, understand the role that God has called your husbands to. He is not only to be willing but to actively die to himself to help you be who God has called you to be. Therefore, you are to reverence/respect your husband like you do Jesus Christ. Most men don't feel any respect in their lives in most areas, so when you show this to your spouse, you will see his love for you increase.

Realize also the moment when your husband makes a mistake and he realizes it, he will also notice that you didn't throw it in his face but will know that you chose to submit and respect him in it. This will demonstrate to his heart that you aren't against him and don't see him as an enemy. This will create a love and loyalty to you that he won't be able to put into words. He will find ways to show you his love all the days of his life.

Realize That You Have a New Teammate

Just like the police officer in the scenario would do anything to protect the woman, men, to what was just stated, you are the front line of defense that God has placed to lead and protect but also to nurture your wife to be all she can be in the Lord.

When working as a team, compromising and submitting to the needs of each other, one of the most important things to remember is that you have a new teammate. A husband and wife need to know that since there is a new teammate, the compromises will be different. The first thing that needs to be done here is communication. You both need to talk about anything and everything.

Little things can bug and eat at a marriage if not discussed. Some of these may be comical and small but can make a huge impact. At the same time, others are big ones that need discussion to avoid pitfalls. These things include the following:

- lowering the toilet seat when finished (men, one wet set down is all it will take)
- the brand of toothpaste or laundry detergent used (yes, I have witnessed an all-out fight over this during marital instruction time with a couple)
- the use of credit cards (this one can be a huge one)
- where to go to church
- how you treat both sets of children if both are parents in the new marriage
- where holidays will be spent
- the need and frequency of sexual intimacy (this can cause all sorts of problems)
- what type of shows to watch—comedy, drama, or sci-fi
- how laundry is folded
- where things can be left—on the dining room table or put away in an office or bedroom
- who gets to park in the garage
- vacation planning

Do you get the importance of communication? The list could go on and on. With this list, there are two important aspects I want to point out.

There Will Be New Ways of Working as a Team

Avoid saying, "Well, that's not the way [ex's name] and I used to do it!"

I can't overemphasize the importance of this one. Underline that with the words "Never say this or even think it!"

If you say this, it is in essence saying that you view the ex-spouse so highly that you want to force the new spouse to follow their same path. Realize you have a new teammate, so everything will start from scratch, whether your previous marriage lasted one year or seventy years. Everything is new, and you need to treat this marriage as such.

In compromising, there are give-and-takes, and communication needs to be the key right from the start. If you are still dating, I encourage you to get everything out on the table at the start so there are no surprises later.

I knew a couple that never talked about children before marriage. Five years into the marriage when she brought it up, he exclaimed that it was out of the question; he never wanted kids in the first place. That was a very important topic to discuss.

Remember—the moment you gave your life to the Lord and got saved, everything was new.

> *Therefore if any man be in Christ, he is a new creature: old things are passed away; behold, all things are become new. (2 Corinthians 5:17)*

In our new relationship with Christ, we don't remind Him of how we liked living in the old life. We can't look back and dwell on the past. Just like in marriage, we have a new teammate, and it is time to walk a new walk together.

In the Christian walk, we are not to keep looking back to the old things.

*And Jesus said unto him, No man, having put
his hand to the plough, and looking back, is fit
for the kingdom of God. (Luke 9:62)*

It is therefore also imperative in marriage to know we don't look back to a previous marriage and how we lived in that one and make the new one conform to it. This marriage is new with a new team player; stop looking back!

Don't Fight Ghosts as a Team Player

The other problem when it comes to compromise is insisting on not compromising a preference in a way that didn't work out with the ex-spouse. Let me use an example that illustrates the point. Let's say in the past relationship, one got involved with a hobby or a form of entertainment such as playing video games. This spouse compromised and allowed it, but then after a time, it took over. They played all day, every day, to the point it got in the way of any family time and even affected work since they would call in just to play.

Well, in the new relationship, the new spouse reveals an interest in video games. If the spouse does not allow this, will not compromise, and fights against it, that is fighting ghosts again. Compromise will not take place in fear of what the old spouse did. Once again, due to fear of the past, the new spouse has to pay for the sins of the old. This is unfair and not healthy. This takes communication from both spouses (refer back to the chapter on fighting ghosts and the portion on triggers).

On the one side, there needs to be a concession and a compromise since this is a new spouse and not the old. On the other side, there needs to be some sensitive understanding on the other part. Once you know that this happens, offer a solution and also some safeguards. In this example, it could be to have play times that don't collide with family needs and quality time; it sets up boundaries.

The important thing is to live in the new day. Don't refuse

to compromise just because someone abused an aspect of it in your past.

My last point on compromise is a very important one.

Do Not Abuse the Love of Your Spouse

I have seen people in relationships who took these biblical principles and twisted them to manipulate their spouse for selfish motives.

When giving marital instruction to a couple, the guy kept saying, "Pastor, you just don't understand." When it was his time to share, he declared everything he wanted her to work on, but she refused to compromise on anything. He then recounted every way he had adjusted and compromised for her, and it was long and extensive. After he said, "I have done all, and she hasn't compromised on anything," she yelled, "Well, you're a Christian husband and supposed to give up everything for me—to even die for me!"

Did you catch the twist and the manipulation of this? He was showing her the love of Christ and was willing to die for her in preferences and wants, but she was showing him absolutely no respect, submission, or love. She was using his role of Christ in dying for her needs for purely selfish motives—to demand and get for herself.

How do you know this has been done to you or you have done it to another? With the list of compromises, if it is always one-sided, with one compromising and the other not budging, manipulation has been done. It is manipulation to such a high degree that God loathes it. It is recorded in the Old Testament and New Testament. Manipulation is right up there with oppression (to lay a heavy burden and crushing weight) and defraud (deprive the personal right to get something from someone).

Ye shall not therefore oppress one another; but thou shalt fear thy God: for I am the LORD your God. (Leviticus 25:17)

That no man go beyond and defraud his brother in any matter: because that the Lord is the avenger of all such, as we also have forewarned you and testified. (1 Thessalonians 4:6)

Therefore, there always must be love and respect.

Realize that this is a sin that God calls out as very harmful and divisive. It takes the love and goodwill of one and uses it for selfish gain. If the other spouse continues in this, it will only get worse.

This takes a life that will get more in line with the Word of God by the Holy Spirit and does whatever it can to show each other great selfless love. It is being totally selfless, just like Jesus Christ. It is having the same mind of Christ Himself.

This whole chapter can be summed up perfectly in these three verses:

Let nothing be done through strife or vainglory; but in lowliness of mind let each esteem other better than themselves. Look not every man on his own things, but every man also on the things of others. Let this mind be in you, which was also in Christ Jesus. (Philippians 2:3–5)

Chapter Seven

Walk in the Light – The Importance of Accountability

> And this is the condemnation, that light is come into the world, and men loved darkness rather than light, because their deeds were evil. For every one that doeth evil hateth the light, neither cometh to the light, lest his deeds should be reproved. But he that doeth truth cometh to the light, that his deeds may be made manifest, that they are wrought in God.
> —John 3:19–21

This is a chapter about which many might say, "Finally, someone is talking about it," and others might say, "We don't need this at all."

Accountability can be a beautiful thing, or it can be a very unenjoyable thing, depending on how you look at it and the motivation behind it. Accountability means the state of being accountable, liable, or answerable; it is a safe place. I will really hit this chapter hard, because if you apply these principles, you will be taking a big step in affair-proofing your marriage.

Take these verses and realize some very powerful truths. First, realize that Jesus is the light of the world.

*Then spake Jesus again unto them, saying, I am
the light of the world: he that followeth me shall
not walk in darkness, but shall have the light of
life. (John 8:12)*

Christ is the light, and there is no darkness in Him at all.
What does light do then?

Light Dispels Darkness

How much light does it take to see? Not much at all; it actually
only takes a spark to be able to see it. Also realize a powerful
truth: darkness really doesn't exist in and of itself; darkness is
the absence of light. When light is shown, darkness flees.

Have you ever been on a cave tour? Many of the tour guides
do this little demonstration where they turn off all the lights to
show how dark it is. Then they turn on a little pen light, and all
attention goes to that little light. It is a good illustration of how
powerful light actually is.

The more of the light of Christ that is in you, the more the
darkness in your life will be dispelled.

Light Reveals Truth

In this passage, it shows that every person that loves darkness
hates the light, because the light reveals the nature of their
deeds; it reveals the truth; it reveals the darkness in which they
live.

Realize that this is one reason people separate themselves
from you as a believer in Christ when you go to a family event
or some social event at work. Understand that, as a believer,
since Christ is in you, His light shines from you as well.

*Ye are the light of the world. A city that is set
on an hill cannot be hid. Neither do men light*

*a candle, and put it under a bushel, but on a
candlestick; and it giveth light unto all that are
in the house. (Matthew 5:14–15)*

Christ's light through you reveals truth in others.
Accountability is a displaying of that light and a response
to that light as well. In fact, let's look at John 3:19–21 again,
and I will show how accountability is seen. Read the same
passage and interject accountability when it says light and
nonaccountability when it says darkness. The truth of this
passage will come to light … pun intended.

*And this is the condemnation, that light is come
into the world, and men loved darkness rather
than light, because their deeds were evil. For
every one that doeth evil hateth the light, neither
cometh to the light, lest his deeds should be
reproved. But he that doeth truth cometh to the
light, that his deeds may be made manifest, that
they are wrought in God. (John 3:19–21)*

Therefore, just as with the light of Christ, it is seen that
accountability in Christ does the same thing. Let's look at what
accountability in Christ does.

Accountability Dispels Darkness

It is plain and simple. Where accountability exists, it keeps
someone from living in darkness. One of the biggest objections
that someone has for accountability is that it says to a person, "I
don't trust you." In fact, anytime a husband or a wife suggests
that they apply some accountability, one spouse usually declares
this objection.

To this, I want to start the answer by gaining an understanding
of how God looks at us. First, there is no one who loves us more
than the Father Himself. There is no one who wants a close,

vibrant relationship with us more than Christ Himself. There is no one who wants to guide us to greater heights than the Holy Spirit Himself. Even though we fail God often, He forgives and then trusts us all over again and again and again to obey and follow His Word.

Now, could you imagine telling God, "If you love me and trust me, then there should be no accountability to You. You just don't trust me!"

We are going to see how God requires accountability, but we'll realize also that trust is something that is earned and grown into as we go throughout life in a relationship. Two people dating will not trust each other as much as two people faithfully living toward each other over a seventy-year marriage. It's that simple.

Realize that even God trusts us more as we are faithful to Him, through the knowledge that we are accountable to Him. If this is true and He knows everything about us, then how much more do we need accountability to establish trust with ones who don't know us as much as God does? Let's look at how God reminds us of how we are accountable to Him.

Let us hear the conclusion of the whole matter: Fear God, and keep his commandments: for this is the whole duty of man. For God shall bring every work into judgment, with every secret thing, whether it be good, or whether it be evil. (Ecclesiastes 12:13–14)

Understand that God is declaring the standard for our relationship with Him and that there is accountability. He is going to bring every work into judgment—all things whether good or bad. God doesn't have to check up on us periodically since He is recording our thoughts, words, and actions every single day, but we will still give an account.

We are accountable even with our very words.

But I say unto you, That every idle word that
men shall speak, they shall give account thereof
in the day of judgment. For by thy words thou
shalt be justified, and by thy words thou shalt
be condemned. (Matthew 12:36–37)

For it is written, As I live, saith the Lord, every
knee shall bow to me, and every tongue shall
confess to God. So then every one of us shall give
account of himself to God. (Romans 14:11–12)

A person who says, "To be trusted means having no accountability," has overlooked God's own pattern for us. Once again, God loves us more than any person has, does, or will ever, but His trust in us grows as we are faithful to Him and the accountability He places on us. Why? Since we know what is expected of us and that we will have to give an answer, it keeps us from doing things we ought not and doing things we ought. Therefore, accountability dispels darkness.

Here is another verse that God gave us to help us be accountable.

For we must all appear before the judgment seat
of Christ; that every one may receive the things
done in his body, according to that he hath done,
whether it be good or bad. (2 Corinthians 5:10)

Did you see that? "Whether it be good or bad." God wants us to know what His will is and keep us accountable to that. This is not an absence of His love and belief in you and me, for His will is always the best for us.

Let me give an example of how accountability keeps our society from darkness. Remember years ago, when a person wanted to get pornography, they usually had to risk driving to an area they normally would never go, risk their vehicle being seen in front of a place where others would automatically know what was going on, then risk the material being discovered by loved ones? This kept many people from getting engaged in and hooked by pornography; this was accountability. There is an old saying that says, "Most people don't resist certain temptations because they are strong; it's just because the opportunity hasn't presented itself." That statement is so true, but with the invention of the internet, smartphones, and mobile devices, there seems to be no risk and therefore no accountability at all.

For many women, if they flirted with an emotional connection with someone other than their husband, they had to risk meeting the person and talking on the phone to have that connection. Now it's as easy as picking up your phone and texting or messaging the other person.

We have created a society that has no accountability, where sin increases, yet people continue to scream, "You should trust me!"

Understand, having no accountability produces a false trust. People go far in hiding the things that they do, such as texting a person of the opposite sex but creating a false contact name of the same sex to hide it, or sending photos to a person and their spouse, so if the photos are discovered, the spouse won't think twice since they will think it was just for them.

Many people who are suspicious of their spouse will not say anything, not because they trust their spouse but because they don't want conflict and are afraid to bring up the concern. This creates a false safety that becomes Satan's playground.

Realize the first one we all need to be accountable to is God. What do we do or not do to be accountable to God? While I won't go into all of what scripture says about it here, I want to encourage you to read, study, memorize, and live the Word of God. Your life will be safe in God, so take these verses to heart. It really makes it simple.

Jesus said unto him, Thou shalt love the Lord thy God with all thy heart, and with all thy soul, and with all thy mind. This is the first and great commandment. And the second is like unto it, Thou shalt love thy neighbor as thyself. On these two commandments hang all the law and the prophets. (Matthew 22:37–40)

Love for God (according to His Word) and others will keep you in His faithful plan. Now look at this verse that promises we have the power and ability to live in Christ.

For it is God which worketh in you both to will and to do of his good pleasure. (Philippians 2:13)

Understand this is saying that God, who is in you, gives you the desire and the ability to do His good pleasure. Wow, what a promise of provision! Let's look at another verse to secure it in our hearts and minds.

I can do all things through Christ which strengtheneth me. (Philippians 4:13)

Let's get into some practical things that bring accountability. Once again, the overriding rule for all conversations setting up accountability is love. Here are some verses from a previous chapter that will help to gain perspective in building trust and love:

Let nothing be done through strife or vainglory; but in lowliness of mind let each esteem other better than themselves. Look not every man on his own things, but every man also on the things of others. Let this mind be in you, which was also in Christ Jesus. (Philippians 2:3–5)

And Jesus said unto him, No man, having put his hand to the plough, and looking back, is fit for the kingdom of God. (Luke 9:62)

You and your spouse can do this in the Lord; look forward and not back! It is love for God and others and a sacrificial selflessness that is the motivation for true accountability. Doing this will produce trust, which we will see more later.

This list of practical ideas is not all inclusive, nor should you, as a couple, approach it legalistically. Pray together and discuss these options and which ones to implement. You may even come up with better ones to implement that would cater more to you as a couple.

If You Can't Do What You're Doing in Front of Your Spouse, Then Don't Do It

This is the easiest practical rule you can follow to keep yourself accountable to your spouse. These following suggestions will help you become more accountable.

Share passwords for phone, mobile devices, computers, all apps, and email accounts.

(Exception would be confidential information for only vocational purposes, but don't use that as a loophole). The internet and social media have created the largest and easiest access to pornography as well as a place where affairs and indiscretions can run rampant.

Pornography can be seen with ease and is a problem that many people have, even within the church. Once again, what was once something that a person had to risk going to a certain area to acquire can now be accessed with a swipe of a finger on a phone in the hand. The access for this is so easy that you must place safeguards up, such as sharing all phone passwords with your spouse, which is the highest accountability.

Social media, once again, has made connecting to people so easy. Checking on past friendships can be good, but many times this also creates a risk to establish past intimate relationships or the temptation to create new ones. Let's be real; some people's curiosity of whether a past love still has a thing for them has caused many to fall for this trap. It usually starts with just likes of posts, waiting to see if the likes are reciprocated. After a while, it then moves to the private message sent that will establish a conversation that tries to build a bridge. It usually moves to sharing cell phone numbers where texts, photos, and videos can be shared secretly with seemingly no ramification. This can include any apps where personal connections can be made, and many are now designed to be extremely secretive and discreet. These connections start out simple then become deeper; they can go from words to photos to recorded video to live video within a short time.

Knowing your spouse has all access to your social media is a way to keep the enemy away from bringing any temptation toward you. Allow complete access whenever asked without any repercussions. Remember accountability will build trust. Think of your spouse wanting to look at your phone not as a breach of trust but as an opportunity to solidify and build trust with them.

Get into the habit and then embrace accountability as an opportunity. If your spouse asks who you are texting or messaging, look at it as an opportunity and let them know. Refusing to tell them and fighting about it because it doesn't show they trust you is a surefire way to destroy any trust they already had in you. Why? Simply put, it is the same reaction as someone who is trying to hide something.

My lady and I established a very good rule, and that is we don't accept any friend invites unless the other spouse approves of it. If they don't, you completely honor the decision. They may have insight from experience or even from God Himself that will protect you.

Another good rule is showing messages received from the opposite sex. Once again, it may be innocent to you, but your spouse may have some God-given insight into the motivation of the other person.

A good example is a guy who was already on my lady's

friend list before I met her. After we started dating, this guy started to message her about how her posts were very inspiring. Now, she does post very good Christian inspirational messages that do edify and encourage, but this guy went from liking to sending a private message. I told her, "Seems fishy. He will probably try to get you involved in a conversation and then start complimenting your looks." Well, it wasn't long, and he started asking her for "spiritual guidance." I knew he was using something (God) that is near and dear to my lady to try to get his (in). Then within a few days, you guessed it, the message. "I just want you to know that you are a very gorgeous woman and I would love to meet you sometime." There it was. It was hard not to say, "I told you so." No, I admit, I did say, "I told you so." So once again, share messages with your spouse and listen to their advice. This will cause a trust that is built on accountability, and Satan himself will not be able to whisper words of doubt in your spouse's ears that will be believed.

Don't be close with a person of the opposite sex besides your spouse.

Some careers may not allow this rule, as long as it is an absolute, have-to situation, such as vocations like EMTs or police officers, but even in those situations, you need to be very guarded. The fact is if you refuse to keep to this rule just because you don't want someone to feel bad or embarrassed that you have this guideline, it is no excuse. Think of this simple fact: there are no physical affairs if the opportunity to be alone with the other person never existed. Keep yourself accountable, free from temptations and from the other person ever thinking there is a chance they can approach you with anything impure.

A note to those who think they are too strong in Christ, or as a person, to withstand the onslaught of Satan that they need no accountability in this area; be mindful of what the Word of God says.

> *Wherefore let him that thinketh he standeth take*
> *heed lest he fall. (1 Corinthians 10:12)*

Understand, God places these warnings in scripture because He knows we need them. He knows we are frail and susceptible to falling. Although, with His power in us, obedience to His Word, common sense, and adherence to accountability, we can live victoriously.

Don't share personal information, especially issues between you and your spouse, with others of the opposite sex or with anyone where an attraction could be made.

This should be the one that common-sense screams for people to avoid, but they don't for the most part. This is where the enemy likes to play. Whether texts, emails, calls, social media, messaging, or in person, run away from this one as fast and as far as you can. The enemy of our souls knows how we are and how we need to have attention, so unfortunately, he arranges temptations for us. One of the easiest ways for Satan to start the temptation is a simple conversation with another about the problems in the marriage. The reason it is such a trap is because it's just a conversation, and it seems so innocent.

When I was a pastor, I had a woman asking me biblical questions through social media. I answered question after question over a period of days. Then she started talking about how her husband wasn't paying attention to her anymore. On one occasion, the woman asked if she could tell me something. I said, "Of course." Her next statement shook me. She said, "I just wanted you to know that you are a very handsome man." It shocked me not only to hear it but also how it made me feel. It was nice to hear. My ex-wife, at that time in our marriage, had stopped talking to me altogether. Realize that these types of conversations bring temptations from the enemy setting you up. Recognize Satan's schemes and avoid them.

Conversations with others of the opposite sex usually hit

during a time when you and your spouse's love and effective communication are at a low point. It will come with thoughts of, *Wow, this person is really listening to me*, or, *Wow, someone cares about what I have to say.*

Remember this passage. It's a warning.

> *In the multitude of words there wanteth not sin: but he that refraineth his lips is wise. (Proverbs 10:19)*

In other words, in the multitude of words, sin is present.

In those conversations, one or both can start to develop an emotional bond with the other person. This is compounded if personal day-to-day issues are shared, especially personal struggles where one may feel they need to start encouraging the other.

It gets worse when one person starts expressing needs that their spouse is neglecting. If you find yourself doing this, whether you know it or not, you are advertising a void for someone to fill in your life. This is opening yourself up to being tempted and tempting the other person to engage in an emotional affair of bonding with you. This causes the words spoken to feel safe, but God is directing us into another way.

> *He that keepeth his mouth keepeth his life: but he that openeth wide his lips shall have destruction. (Proverbs 13:3)*

God wants you to watch what you say and to whom you say it. It may feel safe, and it may have secrecy, but your heart, mind, soul, and emotions are being shared with another other than the Lord and your God-given spouse. This is causing the opposite effect, no matter how it feels, and will lead to destruction.

Realize, if this continues, it will lead to a little flirtation, a little flattery to test the waters. Then, if welcomed, it will lead to sexually charged words and intimate discussions. This will lead to the sharing of photos, videos, and live video chats of a sexual nature. This will bring destruction. Right here I need to interject a passage of warning.

> *But if ye will not do so, behold, ye have sinned against the LORD: and be sure your sin will find you out. (Numbers 32:23)*

God always has a way of bringing out unrepentant sin, in order for us to repent. God says that when we keep our mouth, we keep our life, instead of being in danger of destruction and opening ourselves to marital unfaithfulness, even just emotionally, seek God and His help instead. Run to Him!

> *Set a watch, O LORD, before my mouth; keep the door of my lips. (Psalm 141:3)*

Do not get caught in this trap; don't even start to get lax on accountability. God also gives us a strong warning on this.

> *But I say unto you, That every idle word that men shall speak, they shall give account thereof in the day of judgment. For by thy words thou shalt be justified, and by thy words thou shalt be condemned. (Matthew 12:36–37)*

This is a sobering thought. *Every idle word.* Idle mean useless and frivolous. Even those words are going to be judged, and we will have to give an account for them. They include the words that you say, text, email, and message.

So avoid all temptation to converse in a personal nature with anyone of the opposite sex or anyone you would be attracted to.

Make every effort to have conversations and be very attentive to your spouse. Understand that accountability, like light, dispels darkness from creeping into your life.

Accountability Reveals Truth

And ye shall know the truth, and the truth shall make you free. (John 8:32)

So many people are afraid of accountability because they like their secrets and want a life that has nothing to do with their spouse.

I hope you are getting the fact that when you are freely accountable with your spouse, it builds trust, and we will look at this more from the biblical perspective in a moment.

Accountability reveals truth in a very powerful way. First, let's compare it to a life with no accountability.

False Trust

Once again, when there is no accountability and then one spouse wants to initiate it, the words they will hear are, "I'm so hurt. That means you don't trust me."

Realize what this does; when a person revolts against any accountability, they are doing the very opposite of trust building. They are actually building distrust. Even if nothing ever happens, to avoid building distrust with a spouse, be accountable with them. If a person has nothing to hide, there really isn't any excuse.

Having no accountability develops a false trust. The one who doesn't want accountability thinks that trust has been built, when in actuality distrust has; it's just that the spouse who wants accountability is too afraid to ask anymore, because of fear that it will start an argument.

This can develop a false trust, and they will not ask things that trigger their fear of conflict. Understand, as a pastor, there were times when I would have someone come to me and present instances, things that their spouse was doing that seemed very suspicious. It prompted me to encourage a conversation, whether the fear of conflict was there or not. Some of these circumstances I regularly heard were as follows:

- working late all of a sudden when they didn't before—and getting angry when asked about it
- starting to wearing perfume or cologne out of the blue, but not for special occasions with the spouse
- when the spouse would walk into the room and the other's phone is quickly placed facedown or apps are changed very quickly
- seeing photos of the spouse on the phone that haven't been sent to the other spouse or used on social media
- a sudden interest in a hobby that is completely out of their norm and takes them away from the spouse

The next one can go both ways.

- a total lack of sexual intimacy or a sudden major increase toward it

Let me explain. A total lack of intimacy or engaging in intimacy where there is no feeling or affection from one partner, like there is no interest, could mean they feel guilty when making love to you since their feelings may already be directed toward another. Believe it or not, some get so attached to the one they are having an affair with that making love to their spouse makes them feel like they are cheating on them with their spouse.

Sometimes it is just that the spouse no longer feels emotionally connected because they have been pulling away, but this can be a breeding ground for an affair to start. Major conversations must be conducted, even if you need to seek Christian counseling.

Let me interject here that if there are legitimate health concerns, be sensitive and patient. After some time, if the health concern is over and there is still no interest, then a conversation needs to take place. Another comment though. There are times when the injury or illness may take a long time and unfortunately may last a lifetime. This is something both need to pray and encourage each other through. Affirm your genuine love for each other on a consistent basis. Remember I said this can manifest in two ways. The other way is a sudden major increase toward sexual intimacy. At first, it may seem like a dream come true, but in actuality it may be an indication that an affair or at least an infatuation with someone is taking place. I have heard, as a minister, of instances when the spouse showed a very high increase of sexual desire with their spouse, who later found out they were in the beginning stages of an affair, at least in the emotional stage.

So what's going on in this scenario? They may be on the brink of an affair, or maybe they are fantasizing about someone else, but since the opportunity isn't there, they act it out with their spouse. This may be displayed by it not being personal with the spouse; the actions are there, but there is no genuine affection. Where once there was passionate kissing and little gazes into each other's eyes, now there is no kissing and not even a glance toward the other. Once again, the action is there, but there is a total disconnect from their spouse.

- errand runs increase, and now they must pick up more things that they keep forgetting at the store. Then, what should take just a little time is increased by double or triple the amount of time
- they want to go workout but insist that they no longer want you coming along and almost get angry if you try
- you ask about any behavior change, and they flat-out lie to you, and you catch them in it

This list is not an all-inclusive list, but you get the point. If people are acting a certain way, and it just points to something wrong, something is probably wrong. Do not ignore it; bring it to the surface and have a conversation, whether it starts conflict or not.

The spouse who has guilted the other spouse to never bring something up has created a false trust and is in danger of the enemy to start tempting. False trust and false security will open the door for opportunity. In most instances, when an affair has happened, you will see a progression. It will start with the offending spouse throwing a fit, demanding trust. Then it will progress to having absolutely no accountability in the relationship. Then the offended spouse either blindly trusts or just disengages from the marriage relationship.

When false trust has set in, the following happens:

- no questions asked for getting out of the house alone, since the spouse "doesn't have a right to know"
- spouses sending explicit photos/videos to both the spouse and to the other person so that if they are ever caught with a photo/video before deleting, they have an alibi—no worries about what the spouse thinks
- creating a fictitious contact in the phone for the other person and declaring it as someone from work, church, or a circle of friends; or just creating a second contact name of someone both spouses know, but just off a little so the spouse wouldn't suspect anything even if they saw a notification
- texting or messaging a person of interest while sitting next to the spouse with phone, mobile device, or laptop freely, without a worry that a question will come forth

All of these happen when a false trust and false security have been established and the offending spouse takes advantage of it. Realize, if there was accountability that revealed truth, then the darkness would be dispelled, and false trust wouldn't exist.

True Trust

Look at the beauty of accountability and how positive and beneficial it can be to the marriage relationship.

> *And ye shall know the truth, and the truth shall make you free. (John 8:32)*

In our humanness, sometimes we can't conceptualize how accountability can lead to freedom. I mean, most believe accountability brings shackles of confinement. But think about this question: Confinement from what? The answer to that question is *from what you're not supposed to be doing.* Wow. Powerful realization.

You, as a married spouse, need to know that accountability brings trust. Accountability doesn't bring a trust where no accountability is wanted. Accountability should never stop; there is safety in that and a freedom that will make the relationship stronger.

To prove the point, let us put the marriage relationship in the context of our relationship with God. God holds us accountable for our actions, and that will never stop. He gives us His Word to follow. This is done so we know the truth, and in that truth, we find safety. We know from God's Word what His standard and perfect will for our lives is. Let's see what it does.

> *Thy word have I hid in mine heart, that I might not sin against thee. (Psalm 119:11)*

This truth gets the person who really loves Christ to have a desire to live in Him more, which will bring truth in the inner person, creating a godly desire to please Him.

> *Let the words of my mouth, and the meditation of my heart, be acceptable in thy sight, O LORD, my strength, and my redeemer. (Psalm 19:14)*

Do you see what this is describing? What is this verse asking of God? It is asking God Himself to give you power to live for Him from the deepest part of your soul. It is being accountable to Him. It is living for Him from the very words of your mouth and the meditation of your heart. It is asking God for both to be acceptable in His sight—His righteous and holy sight. It is faith that He will do it, for He is your strength and your redeemer.

Why would we want to be accountable to God in this way? The reason is that He loves us so much and gave His all for us, and therefore, we love Him in return and want to please our Lord and King.

Here is a statement many people may disagree with, but I will back it up: obedience proves your love for Christ.

If ye love me, keep my commandments. (John 14:15)

You may want to read that again if it didn't make you stop in your tracks and think on it.

Would you kick against these truths? No, because they are truth.

Let me ask some questions. Is your wife your wife? Is your husband your husband? You are commanded to love them, and being freely accountable to them displays your love and devotion to them. It says, "I value you enough to be accountable—to keep myself unspotted for you, and for you to live in a trust toward me."

Someone may say right here, "But that is accountable toward God, not someone else."

Well, remember a passage we read earlier.

Submitting yourselves one to another in the fear of God. (Ephesians 5:21)

Through that reverence and fear of God, He wants us to submit to each other; to submit to each other is to provide love, safety and to fulfill needs. Faithfulness is a part of that.

Also, accountability toward God can be lived out as we are accountable to each other. Being accountable means living and speaking truthfully and honestly. Accountability lives in the newness of Christ and conducts itself toward one's spouse.

> *And that ye put on the new man, which after God is created in righteousness and true holiness. Wherefore putting away lying (hiding secrets is lying), speak every man truth with his neighbour (your spouse is your closest neighbor): for we are members one of another (the church, but especially the one you are one flesh with). (Ephesians 4:24–25, parentheses added)*

If you are a new believer, accountability and living truthfully with your spouse is an act of love toward each other. In fact, there is major safety for your marriage that is found in your faithfulness toward God and each other. This is a protection that is strong and will build a wall of protection around both of you so the attacks of the enemy will be thwarted.

Another passage that really gets to the heart of the goal of accountability is in Hebrews.

> *Take heed, brethren, lest there be in any of you an evil heart of unbelief, in departing from the living God. But exhort one another daily, while it is called To day; lest any of you be hardened through the deceitfulness of sin. (Hebrews 3:12–13)*

This living and revealing truth, this accountability, will create trust that nothing can come against or penetrate with doubts.

Once again, does this accountability with God establish more trust? Yes. This trust is built not to get to the point where we are no longer accountable but where we will be more established and proven so that God will grant us more responsibility.

Let's see this trust from God's Word.

> *For the kingdom of heaven is as a man travelling into a far country, who called his own servants, and delivered unto them his goods. And unto one he gave five talents, to another two, and to another one; to every man according to his several ability; and straightway took his journey. Then he that had received the five talents went and traded with the same, and made them other five talents. (Matthew 25:14–16)*

Now the accountability came:

> *After a long time the lord of those servants cometh, and reckoneth with them. (Matthew 25:19)*

What happened through that accountability?

> *And so he that had received five talents came and brought other five talents, saying, Lord, thou deliveredst unto me five talents: behold, I have gained beside them five talents more. (Matthew 25:20)*

This is showing faithfulness, which brought what?

> *His lord said unto him, Well done, thou good and faithful servant: thou hast been faithful over a few things, I will make thee ruler over many things: enter thou into the joy of thy lord. (Matthew 25:21)*

Accountability lived out shows the faithfulness proved, which builds trust, which will open up more blessings.

Understand, one of the things He has given us to be faithful in our marriage is accountability. We need to be accountable to God and each other in the marriage, for when we do, trust grows and allows for more love and blessings from God.

Look at accountability as a blessing and a way to build trust so you will be blessed more in your relationship with Christ and in your relationship with each other as husband and wife. This is a growing process.

My lady and I have established accountability for ourselves and our marriage. Is it easy all the time? No, but knowing it is the will of God, and through His power, we can display our love toward Him and each other more. As we do, we continue to walk in the light of Christ, and even our marriage will be a witness of God's love to a watching world.

But he that doeth truth cometh to the light, that his deeds may be made manifest, that they are wrought in God. (John 3:21)

Chapter Eight

Close All Exit Strategies—Plan for Success, Not Failure

And Jesus said unto him, No man, having put his hand to
the plough, and looking back, is fit for the kingdom of God.
—Luke 9:62

We will borrow from a previous chapter, "Keeping the Peace,"
in that we must pay very careful attention that we don't get
to step 3, the relationship step, in our disagreements. This is
important for every couple on both sides.

Make the Commitment—You Already Did

Speaking from my experiences and my heart, there have been
numerous broken-heart moments in my life. I was not one of the
popular kids in school but rather a middle-of-the-road type of
guy. Since I didn't have any particular group to belong to, there
were times when I felt like I didn't fit in anywhere. When I was
ten years old though, I gave my heart and life to Jesus Christ
as my Lord and Savior. I then dove into the Word of God and
concentrated on growing closer to Him.

Over the years, except for a time when I selfishly walked

away from the Lord and a low time at the end of my first marriage, I was a person committed wholeheartedly to God. That commitment then extended to the person God placed in my life. In the first marriage, there was a promise to not even say the word divorce. That lasted almost twenty-three years before it was said and then filed for. After that, many find themselves in new marriages, where it is easier to throw words around like "divorce," "I don't love you," "I don't even like you," and "It was a mistake to marry you in the first place." These words cut to the heart and unsettle life, as well they should. Remember, as a married couple, even though you are individuals, God still sees you as one flesh.

As previously stated in chapter 2, remarriage is allowed. We addressed the two ways that God allows for divorce (that doesn't disobey the Lord), and that is adultery/fornication (Matthew 5:31–32) and abandonment from the unbelieving spouse (1 Corinthians 7:15).

In both cases though, they are given for an allowance, because Christ knows how hard it is to establish trust again. Even with these allowances, God still doesn't want divorce. His perfect will for every marriage is to work it out with His power.

Therefore shall a man leave his father and his mother, and shall cleave unto his wife: and they shall be one flesh. (Genesis 2:24)

The Pharisees came and asked Jesus about divorce for "every cause." Divorce was so easy and was entered into sometimes without a second thought.

And he answered and said unto them, Have ye not read, that he which made them at the beginning made them male and female, And said, For this cause shall a man leave father and mother, and shall cleave to his wife: and they twain shall be one flesh? Wherefore they are no

*more twain, but one flesh. What therefore God
hath joined together, let not man put asunder.
(Matthew 19:4–6)*

Here we see what God's perfect will is for every marriage, and we need to agree with God's will for it to work. Note here that this is not saying that an abused spouse can't get away for safety and that the offending spouse should not receive help, even if through the law. Understand that separation is allowed in these cases (1 Corinthians 7:10–11).

The Pharisees back then allowed a man to divorce his wife for almost any situation: she got him mad, she said the wrong thing, she showed disrespect, she hasn't kept up with her appearance, she looked at another man, she disobeyed in any way, or the one that many people use today, "I just don't want to be married to her anymore."

This book is for remarriages, and you must overcome everything in your past to work together for this one to work.

The 2016 Census Bureau show the statistics on remarriage and divorce as follows:

- first marriage—divorce rate 41 percent
- second marriage—divorce rate 60 percent
- third marriage—divorce rate 73 percent

It becomes easier with each marriage because God's high view of marriage is lessened in the minds of the persons involved.

With those statistics, we see we live in a similar frame of mind today where no-fault divorces are commonplace. The view of a committed marriage is so low that, once again, there are some people changing their wedding vows from "as long as we both shall live" to "as long as we both shall love." This is a travesty on God's view of marriage. A marriage starting out like this is doomed to failure. In fact, as a minister, I would never perform a marriage ceremony with those vows in it.

Marriage is a commitment between God and each other. This commitment is for life and is not based on pleasant feelings, good finances, steady employment, or the lack of any arguments. Christians, of all people, are to display the specialness in marriage that we previously discussed (Ephesians 5:21–33). The marriage is supposed to display to a lost and dying world Christ's sacrificial and nurturing love for the church and the church's love and respect for Christ. Is it any wonder why Satan does everything he can to erode Christian marriages?

In fact, I believe firmly that demons come out in droves when a Christian husband and wife start arguing, and they add to the intensity by promoting, in that moment, words that hurt, cut, and destroy. Then the pride comes in and refuses to apologize because it may appear weak. So we'll stand our ground and shout out every hurtful thing, declaring, "Well, it's the truth."

Well, think of this simple truth: Christ knows all our hidden thoughts, words, and actions, and in fact, He knows all the sins we have ever done. Therefore, He could stand and declare all of them, leaving you in tears and totally broken, and declare, "Well, it's the truth!" Praise be to God that He doesn't. Instead, knowing the truth, He doesn't pick out the sins and weaknesses but forgives and builds us up in the strength that He gives us.

We need to be more like Christ and let this passage, again, guide our desires and conversations with our spouses. I ask you to read this passage slowly, praying that the Lord Jesus will help you obey it with His power.

Let no corrupt communication proceed out of your mouth, but that which is good to the use of edifying, that it may minister grace unto the hearers. And grieve not the holy Spirit of God, whereby ye are sealed unto the day of redemption. Let all bitterness, and wrath, and anger, and clamour, and evil speaking, be put away from you, with all malice: And be ye kind

one to another, tenderhearted, forgiving one
another, even as God for Christ's sake hath
forgiven you. (Ephesians 4:29–32)

Some of you, if you are honest with yourself, are very mean toward your spouse. I encourage you to slow down and read that passage again. Realize this is God's will for your life as you relate to people, especially the one closest to you—your spouse.

So what are some core reasons people try to create the easy way out, and what do they look like?

They can't catch the biblical idea of
marriage over individuality.

As a pastor, I would never perform a marriage unless I took them through a course to learn the biblical definition of marriage. Once again, when you get married, God takes the two of you and makes you one flesh. It's settled and done. It is not two individuals just starting to become one flesh, but you are one flesh, and God Himself does not want you separating.

Many see marriage in a wrong light; they see it as a simple thing, as easy as God wanting us to be people of truth. Then, if we mess up and lie, we just ask God to forgive us, and we move on. Therefore, if we mess up our marriage, we quickly divorce, then ask God to forgive us and just move on—no worries. That is looking at the divorce as something little and insignificant, and the marriage itself as less than God sees it. God, once again, has such a high degree placed on marriage for what it is a type of, what is represents, and that is the relationship that Christ has with the church.

Therefore, your marriage is not just a piece of paper or just a ring that you slip on. To treat the marriage as low as that is saying that is how little Christ loves the church and how little the church is to be committed to Christ. You are not only cheating yourself, but you are messing up your whole testimony about Christ to a watching world.

Many who can't get over being an individual will also find themselves in an argument, saying, "I don't need you. I'm perfectly okay on my own. I don't need anyone!" Keep this simple fact in mind: Jesus Christ, the Son of God, who is equal with God the Father and God the Holy Spirit, in complete unity in the Godhead, didn't want to feel separated from God the Father. Looking ahead to the cross and knowing there would be a moment when He would feel complete separation, because He would be feeling what everybody would feel when separated from God, He prayed that the cup (representing the sins of the world that would cause this feeling of separation) would pass from Him (Matthew 26:37–44). In fact, once again, this caused Him so much distress that He Himself said, "My soul is exceeding sorrowful, even unto death" (Matthew 26:38b). In other words, he felt so sad that He felt like He could die. This moment was realized on the cross when He said, "My God, my God, why hast thou forsaken me?" (Matthew 27:46b).

Jesus Christ, in all His power, needed and wanted the closeness of God the Father and God the Holy Spirit. He is an individual, but He is an equal part of the Godhead. Resolve that your marriage is a unity of two that have become one. Pray this through, and you will catch Christ's plan and vision for your marriage.

It is highly important to get a greater picture of marriage; it's a *big deal* in the eyes of Christ. It is a commitment that you seal between God and the two of you; it is a life commitment. Make it a commitment to God that from this day forward, your marriage is for life.

This commitment is the one just second to your commitment to Jesus Christ as your Lord and Savior. Understand, you must choose Christ, and the commitment resides in the seriousness of that choice. It is the same as marriage; you choose, and that commitment shows how you view the seriousness of it.

Now, sometimes the spouse can't close the exit strategies because the other spouse doesn't provide an environment where they feel the exits can be closed. If that doesn't exist, then individual living is still the rule instead of one flesh.

Here is what each spouse can do to help close this situation of clinging to individuality:

- Show love in the best way that your spouse—not you— need to feel loved.
- Provide encouragement through life's ups and downs. This is done by keeping communication with your spouse a priority.
- Be the closest friend—the best friend—for each other.
- Foster words of gentleness, grace, mercy, forgiveness, and acceptance.

When a person feels they are sincerely wanted, they are less likely to use words of escape, because they will want to stay in such a marriage.

Here is what each spouse needs to steer away from doing.

Saying words of escape, such as "divorce," "taking a break," "I wish you weren't in my life," "I wish I was alone," "Marrying you was a mistake." These are so far out of the will of God for a marriage that they need to be avoided at all costs. To declare these words are justified because that is the truth that you feel in the heat of an argument does not make them excusable or right. Those words are wrong to declare in a marriage, no matter how you feel. If these are in your vocabulary, you need to pray for God to change your heart.

For out of the abundance of the heart the mouth speaketh. (Matthew 12:34b)

Another reason that someone keeps living with the mindset of an exit strategy is this:

*They feel because of past experiences,
the new marriage is probably doomed to
failure anyway; therefore, subconsciously the
person self-sabotages the relationship.*

It comes to the individual like this – "It's probably not going to work anyway, so I will not invest my heart fully into this." Doing this makes the new marriage not even have the blessing of giving it a chance. In essence, it makes the previous marriage more blessed than the one you just gave your life to. This is done for self-preservation. "I will not allow my heart to be broken, so I will not give myself fully to my spouse." This cheats you, this cheats your spouse, and you will start to use exit terms in hopes that you can get the end started, since it's "probably going to end anyway."

If you are reading this and you are the one self-sabotaging your marriage, and you call yourself a believer in Christ, I implore you to examine your relationship with Christ. This is not God's will for you or your marriage. Jesus says, "What therefore God hath joined together, let not man put asunder" (Mark 10:9). This includes you!

Realize, just like fighting ghosts, you are making your spouse guilty of what a previous spouse has done, but you're also keeping them from your heart, which a previous spouse was blessed with. In essence, not only is your new spouse guilty, but they experience the punishment you want to give to the ex-spouse. This robs your new marriage of the blessed union, safety, and lifelong enjoyment that a marriage is designed for.

Once again, marriage is like Christ's relationship with the church and the church's relationship with Christ. Let's break it down. The church is made up of individuals, so it represents even our relationship with Christ as an individual.

Let's go back to the verse this chapter started with.

*And Jesus said unto him, No man, having put
his hand to the plough, and looking back, is fit
for the kingdom of God. (Luke 9:62)*

Jesus wants complete commitment from us, not a take-it-or-leave-it attitude; that is not commitment. Our commitment is not based on feelings or "our truths" we try to convince ourselves of. If we claim a relationship with Christ, it must be an all-in thing. There is no room for half commitment. This same principle applies to marriages.

Lose self-preservation to keep you from sabotaging your marriage.

Self-preservation is self-seeking, so when you will not give the marriage your all "because it will probably end anyway," it shows an absolute lack of commitment and love, displaying a view that has its highest focus on oneself. At this point, there may be someone saying, "But I just can't. I truly feel that I made a mistake!"

So what! You are married, and at one time, you pledged your love, life, and commitment to that person. God blessed your marriage, and God can bless you in it, if you return to your commitment.

Listen to this very deep truth. If Jesus Christ was all about self-preservation, He wouldn't have ever gone to the cross!

Things were tough. He emptied Himself of some of the glory He had in heaven to come to earth. He clothed Himself with flesh with the limitations that it brought.

> *Let this mind be in you, which was also in Christ Jesus: Who, being in the form of God, thought it not robbery to be equal with God: But made himself of no reputation, and took upon him the form of a servant, and was made in the likeness of men: And being found in fashion as a man, he humbled himself, and became obedient unto death, even the death of the cross. (Philippians 2:5–8)*

In truth, Christ's love and commitment went past feelings. He limited Himself to needing to sleep, eat, and having to go to the restroom. He then endured the ridicule, beating, torture, and death at the hands of people he had made to offer forgiveness of sins. He then rose from the dead to offer victory over death. He became a man to be manhandled. He did all of this based on His love and commitment to us. It went above feelings.

Now, I am not advocating someone stay in an abusive relationship; I said it before. But a separation to bring safety for you and any children involved is needed.

What I'm bringing out is the fact that Christ was committed to us and carried out all that His love and commitment was set out to do—establish and grow a relationship with us.

Can you imagine Christ on the cross? He could have said, "I don't feel this anymore. In fact, making them in the first place was a mistake. It's my truth!" The way of salvation would have ended. Instead, He saw the results of that commitment, which was salvation for us, even through the negative things He had to endure through the process. There is an amazing verse that describes this.

> *Looking unto Jesus the author and finisher of our faith; who for the joy that was set before him endured the cross, despising the shame, and is set down at the right hand of the throne of God. (Hebrews 12:2)*

Did you see that? He looked through the negative and saw the relationship with us; "the joy that was set before him endured the cross."

Marriage is based on commitment to Christ and to each other. Marriage is selfless, meaning you serve the other's needs in building them up.

So look at your marriage how God sees it—a commitment that lasts a lifetime. Seeing it through His eyes will help you be secure in the marriage and not see it as just another relationship that is going to end. This will help you know the marriage is secure, and you won't do anything to sabotage it.

Close Practical Exit Strategies

There are some practical things that people do that make ending the marriage easier. As I go through these, and if you do or have done them, instead of getting mad, ask yourself, "Why am I doing this?" The raw answer will reveal the truth of your motivation. One of the biggest practical ways that demonstrates there is an exit strategy is to not merge finances together, especially when it comes to bank accounts.

When a spouse insists on keeping a bank account totally separate from the other, it usually stems out of an incident in their past, when they were taken advantage of and abused financially. Since we are talking about remarriage, it was usually a former spouse that either drained the finances, made spending decisions without the other spouse, expressed too much control, or mismanaged it, creating adverse financial ramifications and stress.

Finances have been the cause of many arguments and intense feelings in marriages. For the one who insists on keeping finances separate, there is a motivation that, to them, seems right. That motivation is to avoid all the stress and pitfalls that could happen from finances as just stated; it is easier just to keep it separate. They feel that if there is no opportunity to have these difficulties, then there are no worries, and it will keep extra friction from the relationship.

What I am talking about is the spouse who has been financially responsible, with good credit history - keeping everything separate from them reveals two things.

The first thing is that you are still not over the pain of what the last person did, and you are transferring that fear onto the new spouse. This sets the new spouse up as being guilty of what the previous spouse did. Refer back to the chapter on fighting ghosts.

The second thing it shows and says loudly to the spouse is "Just in case this doesn't work, my finances are already protected." This message is unavoidable and is clearly sent. Think of it this way. Say one spouse was very wealthy before the marriage, and one wasn't. One thinks ahead and prepares a prenuptial agreement, because they "don't want to cause stress for the relationship if finances get strained." Now, even though the spouse may say that, and may say it over and over until they believe it, it doesn't change the basic fact that a prenuptial agreement is in place just in case the marriage doesn't work out. The new spouse won't get anything in the agreement, and finances are protected for the other. It is an exit strategy.

Keeping accounts in an individual account apart from your spouse is the same concept. It is an attempt to keep your finances safe just in case it doesn't work; it is an exit strategy. Other exit strategies are keeping property, both real estate and autos, in individual names. Let the title of this chapter sink deep into your heart so that it sparks action. Close all exit strategies.

The exception to all of this is when both spouses agree to any accounts and property being kept in individual names, not because of an exit strategy but to keep taxes down, which could relieve financial stress of the marriage. The important thing is that there still needs to be full disclosure. I know one spouse who had to run their life very tightly, to the point of doing without some needs, because the other spouse was holding funds in a savings account into the tens of thousands. The key to all of this is that both husband and wife completely agree to it.

Keep Hope Alive

I am a person who needs to keep hope alive. If there is not hope, my spirit, mind, and body feel the doom of that reality. The Bible declares this and the reality it plays on our hearts and minds. Let's look at the first part of the verse.

> *Hope deferred maketh the heart sick. (Proverbs 13:12a)*

If one spouse refuses to close exit strategies, it takes the hope out of the relationship and keeps the heart sick in the one trying to hope against hope. After a while, the hoping spouse will just give up to numb the pain until the inevitable happens. This is a human reaction to having no hope.

I remember a story of a town that was going to be flooded by a dam that was going to be built. The project was still two years away, but as soon as all hope was gone from fighting the project, the small town took a downturn. The people refused to do repairs on their homes, ceased to do any landscaping, and stopped manicuring their lawns. The city stopped any improvements on the sidewalks and streets, and maintenance of the city buildings stopped. When asked why they let everything go, the answer that came back was "There is no hope here."

This is the same thing that happens in a marriage when one spouse does not close the exit strategies. The hoping spouse gets the clear picture. They end up shutting down and give up trying. When the hoping spouse loses all hope, the end of the marriage is in sight.

If, however, the spouse closes the exit strategies and sees the marriage as lasting, stable, and growing stronger, hope is restored, and the second half of that verse is realized.

> *Hope deferred maketh the heart sick: but when the desire cometh, it is a tree of life. (Proverbs 13:12)*

Restore and keep hope in your marriage and watch it become a tree of life!

Let Christ Build the Trust

Now one final thing I want to point out is when both spouses are in the process of closing exit strategies. When individualism is being overcome and the belief that the marriage will grow and last sets in, you need to safeguard your heart from doubt and paranoia. Ask Christ to replace those with trust and soundness of mind. Trust the marriage. I mentioned this earlier, but it needs to be said again. It can be applied to both husband and wife. As a man or woman, if you have been cheated on and feel your heart was ripped out of your chest by an ex-spouse who repeatedly said, "Trust me," remember it was your ex-spouse who destroyed that trust. Do not see your new spouse through the lens of the ex-spouse any longer.

Let this passage of scripture be the declaration from God to you both about your spouse. It was spoken of a husband for the wife first, but we will apply it to both.

Who can find a virtuous woman? for her price is far above rubies. The heart of her husband doth safely trust in her, so that he shall have no need of spoil. She will do him good and not evil all the days of her life. (Proverbs 31:10–12)

Keep these things in mind:

- Your spouse is highly valuable to God and to you.
- Both of your hearts can safely trust in each other, and you can be assured you will have no need of good from each other.
- Your spouse will do you good and not evil—no harm all the days of your life.

Trust that God will establish your lives and marriage, and He will bring you soundness of mind and peace to your heart.

Just as you have to believe the character of God and His goodness to you, so you don't believe the lies of the enemy against Him, you need to believe in the character of your spouse and their goodness to you to build a tower against the enemy of your marriage. This will close the exit strategies and make the marriage a safe place to grow closer to the Lord and toward each other.

Chapter Nine

Opposites Attract—
Introverts and Extroverts

Let nothing be done through strife or vainglory; but
in lowliness of mind let each esteem other better than
themselves. Look not every man on his own things,
but every man also on the things of others. Let this
mind be in you, which was also in Christ Jesus.
—Philippians 2:3–5

I need to make a strong point in starting out this chapter before
going into some specifics of introverts and extroverts. There is
something many marriages lack but the strongest ones have,
and that is that both spouses make the marriage a safe place, the
refuge in the storms of life. It is a place where both spouses pour
into the needs of the other. The passage just mentioned gives us
the guidance in what to do in all instances for the other spouse.

When thinking about pouring into your spouse, realize that
one spouse may need more in a particular area than the other.
I am going to lay a general example that if understood will set
the principle for the rest of this chapter.

For instance, one spouse may need affirmation, and the
other not as much. If the spouse does something kind for the
other, and the receiving spouse knows that they want or need

appreciation, they should give it to them. That is unselfish love. The wrong thing to do is to have the mind-set, *Well, they are expecting to be thanked, and I think that's wrong.* Then, based on that mind-set, you give no appreciation.

One spouse may show appreciation for all others in their life but not their spouse. Let me tell you this: the giving spouse is noticing others being appreciated for what they do for them, no matter how big or small, but at the same time they get nothing. This is saying a lot about how the receiving spouse is applying the biblical passage mentioned above.

Christ doesn't withhold anything good from us on the basis that He doesn't need it and, therefore, doesn't think we should need it either. We all come from different backgrounds and have different needs, and we feel loved in different ways, and Christ meets every one of those needs where we are at.

Once you catch the mind of Christ and know what it takes to make your spouse feel loved, to withhold that from them creates a wound that takes healing to get over. Christ can heal your spouse, but realize that He wants to use you to bless them, never harm. He loves your spouse but also wants to love them through you as well. Your goal in your marriage is to draw closer to Christ and to each other. Therefore, make every effort to meet your spouse's need to feel loved.

Once again, we are all different, and opposites attract, so let's look at one way we see this with introverts and extroverts. Let's first look at each one and see how the relation to the other applies.

Introverts

From my experience, I am defining an introvert to mean one who turns inward; a person who focuses attention on oneself; one that dwells on their own thoughts and feelings.

The *Merriam-Webster* 2018 edition defines introversion as "The state of or tendency toward being wholly or predominantly concerned with and interested in one's own mental life."

Let's look at some of the characteristics.

*Introverts are mainly concerned with
one's own state of mind and being.*

An introvert is very reflective and always analyzing life, plans, motivations, and changes. They can spend a lot of time just praying, meditating on God's Word, and thinking with hardly any sensory input at all. They can sit in a quiet room with no noise, and it won't drive them crazy. They also enjoy reading/researching self-help books and other material that focuses on improving self. One main reason that introverts don't share their thoughts of self-awareness with others very much is that self-thinking is one major way that they grow. The amount of time an introvert takes for alone thinking and self-reflecting can vary from a few minutes to an hour or more a day.

A very interesting fact is that Jesus Christ needed this alone time with God to reenergize (Matthew 14:23; Mark 1:35; Luke 5:15–16).

Introverts can be shy but not necessarily all the time.

This point is not a very definitive point; for instance, my lady is an introvert, but she is also in education as a school counselor and is a Christian public speaker for women's conferences. Many times, though, when it comes to small crowds or just a few individuals, her shyness comes out. This can confuse people at times, especially those who have seen her speak publicly. Thus, this point is not definitive.

An introvert can be outgoing when it's a part of their calling, ministry, or vocation, but they are naturally shy and reserved.

*Introverts exert a lot of energy when dealing with
people. Therefore, most of the time they do not
enjoy large crowds and are not particularly social.*

Introverts are very happy just to spend quiet evenings and weekends at home, and they particularly don't like large crowds. The reason for this is that being around people, especially if it requires them to engage, takes a lot of energy from them. In fact, many introverts, if they have a vocation where there is interaction with people most of the day, will arrive home totally depleted of energy. Their energy is built back up with that alone self-reflecting time again.

To an introvert, their home is not particularly a place to entertain others, and you won't find introverts throwing many parties from their home. The home is instead a refuge from the world, a quiet place where they can build up to face the world again. (More on this later.)

Introverts have strong space bubbles.

I didn't know how strong this was until one day when I quickly walked into the living room where my lady was laying on the couch, and I kneeled to kiss her, and her head jerked back with this very surprised look on her face. I was like, "What is that? I'm just trying to kiss you!" To tell the truth, I felt rejected, for it looked like she was repulsed by my sweetness. In truth, it wasn't that at all. At that time, she informed me about her "space bubble," which she hadn't previously prepared me for.

Let me explain. The space bubble for an introvert is a protective area that could be arm's length. This bubble is there all the time, so before any contact, there needs to be a little preparation. This preparation may only take a second or more, but it is a time when they prepare for the bubble to be opened up. It is like you will hear the unspoken words "shields down."

Introverts avoid conflict.

Regular contact with others is draining for an introvert; therefore, conflict is like draining torture for them. Anything that resembles conflict for an introvert will be avoided at all costs. When it comes to most introverts, they will avoid situations or even a tone of voice to avoid a conflict. They will also have a hard time working through conflicts, because it means spending energy to get to the resolution.

During a conflict, introverts may need to take a break for a while, and some may try to not work out the conflict but just gloss over the argument like it never happened in the first place. The only problem with this is that it leaves the conflict unresolved, only to come up at another time.

I have always been an extrovert, and thus I want to quickly work through any conflict and get it over with as fast as I can. In one of our first arguments, while we were about fifteen minutes into it, she blurted out, "This is so exhausting!" To me, it was nothing; we were talking it through. But for her, it felt like torture, because it was draining every ounce of energy from her.

Introverts will do what is needed to try to keep conflicts down, including never speaking about things in a relationship that may start conflict. One thing some introverts need to watch out for is sometimes they feel they can say anything they want and expect others not to disagree with them or be hurt by what they say, because the other individual should know that they hate conflict. We will talk about how an extrovert should interpret this later.

Extrovert's Response to the Introvert

So knowing just a glimpse of the introvert, how does the spouse, who is an extrovert, meet their needs?

Give the introvert alone time.

When I was dating my lady, we would go out, or I would come over around five thirty or a little later in the evening to visit for a few hours. We spent as much time as we could together, and it was marvelous! When we got married, she would go to the bedroom when she came home, lock the door and not come out for an hour or so. I didn't understand why she was doing this. What was the need for this private alone time? It felt like rejection, like she didn't want to spend time with me.

After some conversations and personal study, I found that because of her being an introvert, she came home completely drained of energy from her day. She needed that alone time to reenergize.

The first thing that an extrovert can do is give the introvert some time every day to regain energy, especially after a long day of dealing with people. This should be agreed upon by both spouses and can typically be fifteen minutes to an hour, depending on the severity of the energy drained for the day.

Also, for the extrovert, I would suggest taking this time to do your own private devotions: pray, study the Word of God, and worship. God wants to spend that time alone with you as well.

> *But thou, when thou prayest, enter into thy closet, and when thou hast shut thy door, pray to thy Father which is in secret; and thy Father which seeth in secret shall reward thee openly. (Matthew 6:6)*

Don't force them to be an extrovert; let them be shy.

Another thing that an extrovert needs to do is recognize the shyness of the introvert and not force them into social settings that they strongly don't want to get into (more on the balance of this later). This may seem to make you nuts as an extrovert, but remember it is not about you but about them.

Since you know this, don't make them talk when they don't feel like it. Don't put them on the spot and ask them to tell a story when all eyes are on them, even if you set the story up perfectly. You will hear about it later, and it won't come through shyness! Realize God made them who they are, personality and all. They are marvelously made (Psalm 139:14–15). God made them; you didn't.

Don't force them socially. You may
gently lead them but never force.

As an extrovert, one of the things I love is being social, especially Christian gatherings at church or in a home. One of the plans we discussed early on was to start a house church plant from our home. We set a time for it to start, but as we got closer to the time we were going to start advertising and inviting people to it, I noticed there were things that started making my lady tense. She started asking questions like, "What if they try to investigate other rooms in the house? What if they try to start a full-fledge coffee bar in my kitchen? What if they try to rearrange things or critique me on how I arrange my kitchen cabinets or how I decorate?" I replied, "It's no biggie." This answer didn't sit well.

What I had to do was look at what was going on through her eyes and perspective. Don't get me wrong; my lady loves people, and she is hospitable. But once again, for an introvert, the home takes on a whole other purpose. It becomes the place of refuge, the place where batteries are charged so that they are able to face the world again. An introvert can spend all weekend inside doing nothing and be totally okay with it. In fact, when an introvert says, "Let's go do something," that means their batteries are totally charged!

Once again, this can make an extrovert absolutely nuts; you want to bring people over and entertain. You both need to find a balance in this, but realize your need to entertain is not as strong as theirs is to regain energy to face the world, so have patience and realize your home is the refuge, the place away from the stress of having to live up to other people's standards. It's a place to just be.

Also, make sure you don't force the introvert into large crowds. If you have any type of gathering that will have a crowd, the simple thing is to allow the introvert time to prepare and also to give them their quiet time, if needed, before the event to energize.

I mentioned there should be a balance with social activity,

and we will discuss more about this when we talk about socializing when it comes to extroverts. The important thing is not to force them but to gently lead them into this balance.

Respect the space bubble.

Not a lot has to be said about this one, except to remind you not to take it personally and do your best not to feel rejected. The only time you would need to question the space bubble is if you see others invading that same bubble by surprise, and you see no wincing or recoiling from the introvert. If you notice that it is only with you, some serious questions need to be asked.

Besides that, though, respect the space bubble. There are ways you can let them know when you're going in for a hug or a kiss. The best way is let them see you coming. I even catch myself, since I surprised my lady, by stating, "I'm coming in for a kiss." She sometimes finds this silly, but I know how I felt rejected (even though that's not what she did), and so I do what I can to make sure I don't feel that pain again and to make her comfortable as well.

Be as nonconfrontational as you can be.

This is a big one when it comes to introverts and extroverts. This one you will definitely need God's guidance and help with.

As an extrovert, you see conflict as the symptom of a root problem that you want to fix. You will have to pray for wisdom and patience. Yeah, yeah, I know. Patience is hard to pray for because God gives you opportunities to learn it!

An extrovert can be very vocal. They may lift their voices more and have large gestures, and those can be taken like they are starting a conflict, when sometimes it's just the way they are. (More on how introverts react to this later.)

The important thing to note here (and I'm still learning it) is when something is said to an extrovert that would normally be considered as a challenge from another extrovert, it is not so from an introvert. Remember they hate conflict.

Let's take a simple example. Maybe an introvert says, "Tell me—why did you take that action when that happened?" You, being the extrovert, interpret that as a challenge with a presupposition that your choice was wrong and the introvert is grilling you to prove to you that you made the wrong decision. Now, that may be true of some people but usually not from an introvert. The introvert is asking the question not to challenge you, but they genuinely want to know the answer, because they want to understand. This, if not understood, can cause you, the extrovert, to escalate it into a conflict, which is not what the introvert wants at all. Remember they want to avoid conflicts almost at all cost.

There have been times in our marriage when my lady has gotten quiet with me and not talked for a while. When I would ask, she wouldn't respond, for fear that anything she said would resemble an attack or an invitation to a conflict, which is what I was doing to make her get quiet in the first place.

It can be a vicious cycle that extroverts don't even know they are doing—interpreting everything through the lens of the other trying to attack, start a conflict, or prove that they are wrong.

What happens? Extroverts tend to be very loud and boisterous and are quick to show emotions. Therefore, the conflict can be escalated quickly. If they get to the point that the introvert is yelling back, they should see the danger lights flashing. Many times, extroverts don't though; instead, they keep pushing through, because they feel that the only way the conflict will be over is if they work through it all the way, right now. Here is the problem with that thought. The introvert hates conflict, and they hate getting angry even more, because it takes every ounce of energy they had to try to stay calm. Then, in the anger, their energy gets depleted even more than they can handle, creating a very strong negative memory for the introvert. The introvert needs some time to calm before reaching that point, and definitely afterward, and maybe you, as the extrovert, need it as well. Now this time should be minutes or an hour or so but not days, for that doesn't line up with scripture (Ephesians 4:26–27).

An extrovert can go through a conflict and quickly kiss and make up, but an introvert, through the fight, can almost feel traumatized by it. It may take hours, days, weeks, or sadly months for them to see you without seeing the trauma that was created. To you, it was just a fight, but to them, it could have felt like an internal world war. Much prayer, gentleness, understanding, and sometimes time is needed to heal these wounds.

Here are some verses I want you to meditate on and internalize. I will not provide commentary for most but let the Holy Spirit illuminate them for you.

> *Keep thy tongue from evil, and thy lips from speaking guile. Depart from evil, and do good; seek peace, and pursue it. (Psalm 34:13–14)*

> *Cease from anger, and forsake wrath: fret not thyself in any wise to do evil. (Psalm 37:8)*

> *He that keepeth his mouth keepeth his life: but he that openeth wide his lips shall have destruction. (Proverbs 13:3)*

> *He that is soon angry dealeth foolishly: and a man of wicked devices is hated. (Proverbs 14:17)*

> *He that is slow to anger is better than the mighty; and he that ruleth his spirit than he that taketh a city. (Proverbs 16:32)*

> *The discretion of a man deferreth his anger; and it is his glory to pass over a transgression. (Proverbs 19:11)*

Whoso keepeth his mouth and his tongue keepeth his soul from troubles. (Proverbs 21:23)

Wherefore, my beloved brethren, let every man be swift to hear, slow to speak, slow to wrath: For the wrath of man worketh not the righteousness of God. (James 1:19–20)

If any man among you seem to be religious, and bridleth not his tongue, but deceiveth his own heart, this man's religion is vain. (James 1:26)

For he that will love life, and see good days, let him refrain his tongue from evil, and his lips that they speak no guile. (1 Peter 3:10)

The next verse is one that we should all remember in an argument.

A fool uttereth all his mind: but a wise man keepeth it in till afterwards. (Proverbs 29:11)

In an argument, we usually spill out everything in our mind and all our feelings. Have you ever said, "And another thing!"? That is what this verse is speaking about.

Another great set of verses to obey when addressing another believer and especially your spouse is the following:

Let no corrupt communication proceed out of your mouth, but that which is good to the use of edifying, that it may minister grace unto the hearers. And grieve not the holy Spirit of God, whereby ye are sealed unto the day of redemption. Let all bitterness, and wrath, and anger, and clamour, and evil speaking, be put away from you, with all malice: And be ye kind one to another, tenderhearted, forgiving one another, even as God for Christ's sake hath forgiven you. (Ephesians 4:29–32)

Even in an argument, remember two things. The first thing is the other believer is a temple of the Holy Spirit (1 Corinthians 6:19–20), so if you are tearing each other down, you are grieving the Holy Spirit. The second thing to remember, even in the argument, is to be kind to each other, to be tenderhearted and forgiving, even as God, for Christ's sake, has forgiven you.

Protect your marriage.

You know what the introvert's needs are, what will make them feel loved, valued, and wanted. At the end of the day, the introvert needs to know that their spouse loves them and knows them through and through. They need to know they are safe with you and can talk about and share anything with you without conflict. They spent all day at work getting their energy drained, so even though they get energized by being alone, also help them see you as the one who builds and edifies them in a safe way; you will have a friend and spouse who will know that you are a blessing.

Now, let's look at the opposite of the introvert.

Extroverts

Once again, by my experience, I am defining an extrovert to mean one who turns outward. They focus attention on others and feel satisfaction investing in and interacting with others.

The *Merriam-Webster* 2018 edition defines extroversion as "The act, state, or habit of being predominantly concerned with and obtaining gratification from what is outside the self."

Let's look at some of the characteristics.

Extroverts are mainly concerned with others and are outwardly focused.

Over the years, extroverts have been the brunt of many introverts' blogs and articles out there on social media. The call has been given for extroverts to understand introverts (which they should) but with an almost completely negative view of who they are, like being an extrovert is wrong or weak somehow.

Many articles display being an introvert as the strong one because they get energized by self-awareness, and extroverts are displayed as weak because they get energized by being with others. This has been interpreted as "sucking energy from others," which is not the case. Extroverts gain energy by being with and serving others. For instance, they like to see and make others laugh. There are hardly any introverted comedians.

Extroverts like to see someone enjoy something they did for them. When an extrovert does a service, gives a gift, or does anything for another, they get charged by helping and serving the other person.

Extroverts love supporting and encouraging others. When an extrovert is married to an introvert, it can present many challenges. Introverts, because they are self-aware, can tend to also be ultra-individualistic. Why does this present a problem? The reason is when the extrovert offers encouragement and support, the introvert sometimes interprets it wrongly—that they are telling them that they are not strong enough to handle things by themselves.

Here's an example. My lady was going through something, possibly medical, and I said, "Well, I'm praying for you, and I'm here for you no matter what." Her reply was "Thanks, but I'm not looking for that." Now, to an extrovert, that felt like a rejection of my goodwill and my very character. She didn't mean it that way at all; remember she is self-aware and self-reliant. That is why introverts and extroverts need to see life from each other's point of view.

What is interesting also is that extroverts do very well

in service careers, such as ministry (although my wife is a great minister, so this is not cut and dry), politics, teaching, marketing, nonprofits, the medical field, police, and emergency responders. They thrive by being there for others, and they get satisfaction in life from this.

Extroverts are bold and assertive.

The phrase "silence is deafening" rings true loud and clear for the extrovert. Remember that an introvert energizes by being alone and self-aware, whereas an extrovert energizes by being around others.

Whereas introverts are mainly shy, extroverts are bold. They don't have trouble talking to strangers and making friends fast. They are assertive in social gatherings and have no problem approaching new people. For instance, not only do extroverts do well in service occupations, but they also do well in sales and customer service occupations. Extroverts are what we call people persons. They get bored easily and like life to be in motion.

Extroverts gain energy by interacting
with others and are very social.

Extroverts typically can spend time alone and handle it, but they would rather be with others. When spending time with others, they also want to be social with interaction. They can be in a room with their spouse watching a movie but at the same time will enjoy interaction, even if it is just holding hands, speaking when they can, or any interaction at all. To an extrovert, sitting in a room with someone they don't even know and not being social is just plain awkward. In this case, after a while, some interaction will be made; if not, social media will be utilized to fill in the awkwardness of the situation.

Once again, the important thing to realize is that they get energy from being around other people—not to drain the energy from them but to gain energy from interacting with them and serving them any way they can. Their motivation is to encourage and to uplift, which makes them feel very fulfilled. Extroverts are not selfish, as many social media articles portray them to be. Once again, that is a total mischaracterization of them and their motivation. In fact, since extroverts are others centered, it could be argued they are selfless instead.

Extroverts love contact connection.

From the first look to holding hands with the spouse, the extrovert thrives on this. Unlike the introvert that has a space bubble, the extrovert does not. Even if an extroverted guy has another guy friend surprise him with a bear hug and a light tackle, it is not hated but embraced—well, unless it was a hard tackle to the ground maybe.

When speaking about their spouses, they welcome any contact with their spouse; it really does relay feelings of friendship, intimacy, and love.

There is a point that needs to be made here, and that is the extrovert holds in high esteem the ones let in for the contact connection. They love for their spouse to reach out and embrace them warmly, give them long, lingering hugs and kisses, and be intimate with them. Therefore, if you are an introvert and you have a space bubble, you need to allow your spouse, who is the extrovert, to come in; but not only that, make sure that they are welcomed in. To let them into your bubble for only a few seconds a day would be the same as for them to only allow you a few seconds a day to not be in your bubble. More on the balance of everything a little later in this chapter.

Extroverts want to work through conflict.

The Bible has much to say on conflict resolution, and one high command—yes, I said command—is found in scripture.

> *Be ye angry, and sin not: let not the sun go down upon your wrath: Neither give place to the devil. (Ephesians 4:26-27)*

This is one passage extroverts thrive in, because it meets them where they are at. Extroverts want to get over a conflict as fast as possible. A note to introverts to understand something very deeply: when an extrovert feels at peace with you, and they can have very pleasant interaction with you, that is what satisfies and energizes them the most. Think about it. If an extrovert is just trying to suck your energy, then wouldn't it make sense they would be emptying themselves of their fuel supply? This would be counterproductive, especially in an argument.

Their goal is not to take your energy but to get to the point you will feel better and the bridge is mended between the two of you as quickly as possible. Your energy and their energy could be replenished faster is the thought. We already addressed the introvert side of this, so understand that the extrovert is wanting this conflict to be worked out quickly.

Besides, both of you can learn to be angry and not sin, and with all that is in both of you, you can make sure that the sun does not go down on your anger. Do not go to bed if there are hurt feelings between the two of you. Neither one of you should just say, "I'm not mad," and storm off to bed. If feelings are heightened with either one of you, work it out, at least to the point that the feelings are not so tense before you both go to bed. Why is this so important? As mentioned in a previous chapter, if you go to bed on it, thinking of it, you may have dreams of it, and more than likely, you will wake up with it on your mind, and then sometimes you'll go throughout your whole day rehearsing it. Doing this gives the devil time to try to give himself a place to make inroads. His goal, of course, is to destroy the marriage and your very soul. Don't let him do it!

An Introvert's Response to the Extrovert

Now that you have seen some of the corresponding characteristics of the extrovert, let's look at how the spouse, who is an introvert, can meet their needs.

Share your time with the extrovert.

The extrovert was encouraged to give you alone time to reenergize and gain strength, but you need to give them time needed with you as well. Hopefully by now, you have caught that they aren't sucking your energy but that they want to spend time with you to invest in you, which energizes them and brings satisfaction. There needs to be balance. Don't expect the extrovert to give you agreed-upon alone time, and then the only quality time you give them is a quick question, "So how was your day?" Then as soon as they answer, you act like you gave them the needed quality time. Neither is quality time sitting in the same room and being on the internet, social media, or messaging your other friends. It should be time when, even if you are doing an activity, there is a concerted effort to enjoy each other in the activity. Whatever you do during this time, don't give your spouse a disgusted look because they "interrupted you" if they want to engage with you.

I will address this more later, but your spouse, the extrovert, gains energy by serving and interacting with you, so don't starve them when you are together. You are the one they want to invest in the most, so don't let them, every day, return home only to be made to feel unwanted or rejected.

Remember it is not about you and your wants. You are not commanded by God to serve yourself but rather the other, and the closest one is your spouse. Let them know that, of all people in your life, they are the most important one you want to spend your time with, and actually do it!

Don't force the extrovert to be shy like you; embrace their boldness.

Introverts are by nature shy and private; they feel that if nobody knows anything about them, the better. An extrovert is not built that way. They want to engage in meaningful conversations, starting or carrying on a friendship with meaningful dialogue. They want to learn about the other person they are talking to and want to share information about their lives as well.

Remember they are bold and assertive. To tell an extrovert when going to a social gathering, "Now, don't share anything about our lives, whatsoever," is paramount to saying, "You may as well put duct tape on your mouth when we get there and not talk at all."

So how do you work with this? It is easy. Extroverts are already good at talking and learning about the other person, because they want to get to know them, so the other part is to discuss and agree on the details about your lives together that you consider off-limits. Clear discussion as a couple will really go a long way in setting up boundary subjects and how much of a subject can be shared. This will save stress for the introvert and prevent an argument afterward, keeping the extrovert from feeling ridiculed for just being who they are.

One last thing. Extroverts, because of their boldness and assertiveness, can just be silly and weird. I know, I am one. So let the extrovert be that with you and laugh some. It's probably one of the reasons you were attracted to them in the first place.

Go with the extrovert to social events.
Don't force them to be nonsocial.

Some may think, *Well, they can do what they want, but I won't go.* That is a recipe for disaster. Remember the extrovert wants to do things socially but wants to do them with you. You are their favorite person, and you are a part of their socializing. There needs to be a balance. I am not saying you have to go out every night of the weekend, but have a candid discussion with your extrovert spouse about going out. Remember both need to concentrate on each other's needs, so make sure the extrovert has time to be social, with you along.

Being alone with themselves and God is something an extrovert needs to be able to do, and you can encourage them in this. At the same time, realize God knows we all need interaction with others. Even though scripture talks about being alone with God in the "prayer closet" (Matthew 6:6), it also talks about how we need to be with others as well.

And let us consider one another to provoke
unto love and to good works: Not forsaking the
assembling of ourselves together, as the manner
of some is; but exhorting one another: and so
much the more, as ye see the day approaching.
(Hebrews 10:24–25)

We need others; we need edification and encouragement, and we need to provoke each other to love and good works. Realize, when it comes to scripture, God calls every person that He made to different parts in His body; it is all balanced in that God sees life as a connection of others and not isolation to the introvert or extrovert. There is no better way to live this balance than in a marriage that enjoys life and each other—introverts and extroverts joined together.

Love on your extrovert.

Even though you, as an introvert, have a space bubble, your extrovert does not. There are some things they would love! Keep in mind you can do these things without them initiating them: grab their hand and hold it, give them a long hug and show them you enjoy it, kiss them, and yes, sometimes passionately! Place your hand on them for no apparent reason, such as when you are watching a movie or riding in the car. Find times to make the extrovert know you love them through touch.

If you have contact with them only when they initiate it and you let them into your space bubble only by permission when they approach first, it will cause them to wonder about your desire for them. Once again, don't allow the enemy to do anything to create doubt. One way the enemy tempts is to get them to doubt the love of the spouse.

Intimacy between a husband and wife is not something to be tolerated; it is a beautiful gift that God has given for you both to enjoy. Therefore, introvert, approach your extrovert with your affection and meet their heart's need.

Start working things out through the conflict.

It is impossible for a husband and wife to never fight (see previous chapter on fighting well), but the conflict can be kept to a minimum.

In the first place, don't expect the extrovert to get into a conflict and be quiet and reserved because they should know you don't like conflict. That is not their character. There is a difference in being mean and being animated; you need to learn the difference. Remember the extrovert is bold and assertive, so in an argument, don't assume they are going to be docile and quiet. I'm not talking about being abusive; that you must get away from. Understand though that the extrovert strongly desires to work through the conflict as fast as possible, and being passive, to the extrovert, will not work.

Since we know God wants the conflict to be worked through, do it. If you need to step away for a moment, do so but not with last hurtful words as a jab, for this does more harm than good. At the same time, make sure this time is to calm yourself, not as the start of a silent treatment against your extrovert. Sometimes this turns into hours and then carries over to the next day or goes on for days at a time. Introvert, this is not calming time unless you have such a problem with anger that it takes that long to calm, and if so, you need to be in prayer, seek out scripture and Christ's help. Many times when the cold treatment is extended, and you know it's hurting the extrovert every minute you aren't talking to them, realize you are punishing them. In truth, you are continuing to hurt their heart and creating a rejection wound that will take Christ Himself to heal. That is why God doesn't want the sun to go down on your anger.

Once again, review the previous chapter on fighting well. Remember to work with each other to end the conflict, to get to the other side and continue to grow closer to Christ and each other.

Protect your marriage.

Know what the extrovert's needs are that will make them feel loved, valued, and wanted. Many times, you, as an introvert, come home drained, and even after some alone time to reenergize, you still carry on the rest of your evening not wanting to talk or engage with your spouse. Remember— even if the extrovert has been around people all day, they are looking forward to coming home all day. Why? Remember what energizes them is to encourage, spend time, and serve you, their favorite person. When they get home, before or after your quiet time, let them have that quality time with you. You both are the most important person to each other; therefore, quality time together is the only way your relationship will grow.

Realize if you, as an introvert, don't give them what they need and desire—quality time with you—then the extrovert will naturally make assumptions. First is that you, the introvert, are spending all your best time with others. The extrovert knows that all the interactions, all the smiles, all the laughs are being used for others. This leaves the extrovert starving for you and even envious of others.

The second thing this will do is make the extrovert feel they aren't worth seeing or spending energy on, that they just aren't worth it. Be very careful of this because if the extrovert is helping to give you time alone to restore your energy, and you don't reciprocate, then you are saying they need to get their energy and satisfaction from interaction with others. The extrovert wants and needs you.

Let them know, besides Christ, they are the most important person in your life. Actions speak louder than words.

Final Thoughts

In ending this chapter, I need to leave you with some final instructions.

This is a beautiful thing when both the introvert and extrovert apply this passage to their lives and their relationship.

> *Let nothing be done through strife or vainglory; but in lowliness of mind let each esteem other better than themselves. Look not every man on his own things, but every man also on the things of others. Let this mind be in you, which was also in Christ Jesus. (Philippians 2:3–5)*

* Esteem your spouse better than yourself.
* Look not at your own needs but the needs of your spouse.
* This takes on the mind of Christ. It is selfless.

There is not any time when one spouse demands that their needs be met while doing nothing to meet the needs of the other. This forces them to spend energy they just don't have. It is selfish, it is cruel, and that is not the mind of Christ.

The beautiful thing is when both spouses work on meeting the needs of the other. When this is done, you won't have to worry about your energy or your needs being met; it will happen automatically.

> *For he that soweth to his flesh shall of the flesh reap corruption; but he that soweth to the Spirit shall of the Spirit reap life everlasting. And let us not be weary in well doing: for in due season we shall reap, if we faint not. (Galatians 6:8–9)*

Therefore, if you serve Christ by sowing the needs of your spouse, you will reap of the same and both of you will be edified.

Also, don't grow weary but keep it up; you will reap not only spiritual blessings from God but also a blessed marriage where both are built up closer to Christ and each other.

Chapter Ten

Be Jesus to Each Other

> So after he had washed their feet, and had taken his
> garments, and was set down again, he said unto them,
> Know ye what I have done to you? Ye call me Master
> and Lord: and ye say well; for so I am. If I then, your
> Lord and Master, have washed your feet; ye also ought
> to wash one another's feet. For I have given you an
> example, that ye should do as I have done to you.
> —John 13:12–15

Your Spouse Is the One You Will Minister to Most

This chapter is really a continuation of the last chapter. It will
fly against the grain of many because we don't want to be like
Jesus in many areas of our lives. Once again, both spouses
need to be committed to serving each other and filling each
other's needs. One spouse can't demand to be served but not
do anything for the other; that is manipulation and far removed
from the heart of Christ. If both live to fulfill these needs, then
each one will be filled, and the marriage will grow.

I titled this chapter "Be Jesus to Each Other" because I have
seen many couples—and if you have been divorced, you've

seen it—where one person seems to be kind, loving, and nice to everybody else, even to a stranger, but not toward their spouse. I have also known couples where one spouse is constantly helping others and doing ministry, all the while ignoring the spouse who is needing, even starving, for their affection. Let's talk about this very important aspect.

Be Jesus to Your Spouse First

But from the beginning of the creation God made them male and female. For this cause shall a man leave his father and mother, and cleave to his wife; And they twain shall be one flesh: so then they are no more twain, but one flesh. (Mark 10:6–8)

You are one flesh with your spouse. Therefore, to love your spouse is loving yourself in the long run. In fact, let's look at a verse directed toward husbands to see this biblical reality.

So ought men to love their wives as their own bodies. He that loveth his wife loveth himself. (Ephesians 5:28)

Therefore, you as a couple are one flesh. The one who needs your Christlike characteristics and ministry first and foremost is your spouse. Realize that this simple fact, if neglected, will lead to the end of countless marriages and many children left with confused and hurt feelings for many years. If you invest in others because you feel God's calling and leading but don't first minister to your own spouse, you are disobeying God's call for ministry. If you can't say amen, say ouch!

Let me give you an example from a young man I worked with at a fast-food restaurant when I was a teenager. We were talking about God and church, and he became very agitated and even physically red in the face with anger. When asked why it made him so upset, he proceeded to tell me that his dad was so bent on helping and ministering to others that he saw his mom and his siblings do without. When it came to quality time, his dad was never there for them, because he was always out helping others. Even when his mom would beg for his time, she was told that God was first and serving others was the calling.

One memory that really stood out for him was when he and his siblings needed shoes because theirs were falling apart. Another family in the church was in the same predicament, so his dad bought all new shoes for the other family's kids, while they had to do without. When they complained, they were told they needed to sacrifice for others. This caused this young man to have ill feelings toward God, his father, and the church. His father didn't have a good understanding of God's Word, will, or calling.

Another example is from a woman who was married but bragged that she always put her kids first, no matter what. Unfortunately, the husband was put on the back burner for many years until the youngest was around nineteen years of age. He had waited all those years, begging for the wife's time and affection. They never even had a date night unless it was to go do or get something for the kids. When the empty-nest time started, the husband thought this would be the time to have his wife's attention and quality time, but sadly, the years of not concentrating on each other led to the fact that they were parents but not friends. She didn't know him as her husband, only as the father of her children. Within a year, she left, and he received divorce papers. The reason—she didn't know him and felt that she no longer wanted to take time to get to know him again. She concentrated all her time and attention on her kids that would one day be gone and didn't realize she was losing her best friend.

Understand that your spouse comes first, even before your kids. The reason is the kids will move away someday, and your spouse will be the one who is left. If you have the love and friendship going the whole time and growing closer to each other, then you will have the life partner to enjoy the freedom with, apart from the parental constraints that you had. Life can continue to be very enjoyable.

Even if you both have kids from previous marriages, this concept becomes of even greater importance for you. Many times, a new spouse will hear, "My kids were before you came along, and they will always be before you." I have even heard a spouse say, "My kids are my constant, and you can be replaced." Realize, if you want resentment between your spouse and your kids, that's the perfect way to do it. You have set the marriage up for failure either when the kids are still around or when the empty-nest starts.

Understand something very spiritual and impacting about your marriage to your spouse. Even though your children are blood, your marriage in God is closer and more powerful, because only with your spouse are you one flesh (Matthew 19:5). That spiritual bond can never happen with your children, for it wasn't designed by God to be. Being that marriage is the highest relationship according to Jesus Christ on planet Earth, it is your responsibility to have as high of a view of your marriage as God Himself does.

Also, when it comes to meeting needs and being Jesus first to your spouse, let's look at a very strong verse about those in our household, especially our spouses. This can be applied to both husband and wife.

But if any provide not for his own, and specially for those of his own house, he hath denied the faith, and is worse than an infidel. (1 Timothy 5:8)

Being Jesus first to your spouse is providing the needs of your own house. This is to take precedence over all other relationships. If not done, the person is worse than an infidel— meaning an unbeliever.

There are other passages that show that focusing your attention on your spouse as the first priority in relationship is God's will; these passages are Ephesians 5:21–6:4 and Colossians 3:18–21. The spouse is the first person you concentrate on in your life, even before children. There is only one person in your life who is your helpmeet, and that is your spouse (Genesis 2:18).

Love Your Spouse Like Jesus Would

> *Jesus said unto him, Thou shalt love the Lord thy God with all thy heart, and with all thy soul, and with all thy mind. This is the first and great commandment. And the second is like unto it, Thou shalt love thy neighbour as thyself. On these two commandments hang all the law and the prophets. (Matthew 22:37–40)*

Look at that. Love your neighbor as yourself. Your spouse is the closest neighbor to you! Don't attempt to be loving and kind to others you know and even strangers if you are unloving and unkind toward your spouse.

It was eye-opening when I would talk to couples that needed scriptural instruction for their marriage. I would ask them, "Do you think your spouse loves you?" I usually got back, "Yes." I would then ask, "Does your spouse like you?" Many times, I received the answer, "Oh, no."

At that point, one spouse would start listing the reasons not to like their spouse. It was usually a long list of things they had already worked on that one was still holding against the other.

After that, I would say, "Imagine God wrote a list and mentioned every sin that you have ever done against Him and everything that you are doing that may be disappointing Him. I'm sure it's a whole lot more than your spouse has ever done against you. Now, how would you feel if God said, 'I love you, but to tell the truth, I really don't like you,' then brought up all those reasons that were on your list? Let me ask, how would that affect you in your relationship with God?" Many times, I would get the answer, "Defeated, unwanted, unworthy, unloved, and despised." I would then ask, "When you say to your spouse, 'I love you, but don't like you,' and then list the reasons, how is that supposed to make them feel?"

Understand, Christ has a high command for how we are to love. Look at this radical passage.

> *But I say unto you, Love your enemies, bless them that curse you, do good to them that hate you, and pray for them which despitefully use you, and persecute you. (Matthew 5:44)*

God commands us to do certain things for our enemies. What is an enemy? The definition can be seen in this verse; it is someone who curses you, maybe even your very existence. An enemy hates you and fosters no good will toward you. They also despitefully use you and even persecute you.

For this enemy, who is against everything you are, Christ wants you to love them, bless them instead of curse them, do good to them instead of hate them, and pray for them.

Here is the question you need to ask yourself: If you are supposed to react this way to someone who hates your very existence, how do you think God wants you to treat your spouse, the very one He made you one flesh with? The answer to that question is rather obvious. Stop seeing your spouse as your enemy and see them for who they are. Love them a whole lot more than you are commanded to love an enemy. Start there. Love your spouse like Jesus would.

Love Your Spouse Sacrificially Like Jesus Would

"I'm not giving anything up for them!" One may say something like this, but understand that type of heart does not have the love of Christ dwelling in it. The love of Christ doesn't demand but sacrifices to meet the needs of the spouse. Christ sacrificed Himself out of joy, through His love, not out of a demand from Him. Take a look at the love of Christ.

> *Hereby perceive we the love of God, because he laid down his life for us: and we ought to lay down our lives for the brethren. (1 John 3:16)*

Christ's love is our example, and we should not see our spouse as one we need to stand up against but as one we serve sacrificially.

> *This is my commandment, That ye love one another, as I have loved you. Greater love hath no man than this, that a man lay down his life for his friends. (John 15:12–13)*

Christ wants us to love just like He does, and that means sacrificially—even to lay down one's life for a friend, and your spouse is your closest friend. If He desires us to be willing to lay down our very life, then we can lay down any of our selfish desires to meet the needs of our spouse. Determine today, right now, to love your spouse as Jesus does.

Serve Your Spouse Like Jesus Would

Wow. What? Serve your spouse? What? Yes, I said serve your spouse and meet their needs.

Remember, in a previous chapter, we covered submission. Let us revisit a verse, and then we'll see how to apply it.

> *Submitting yourselves one to another in the fear of God. (Ephesians 5:21)*

We need to understand this is talking about meeting the needs of the other. The husband is called to submit to the needs of the wife, and the wife is called to submit to the needs of the husband. When you got married, the day of living just to satisfy yourself was over. Remember the marriage is the example of the relationship between Christ and the church. Once again, let's see how Christ serves.

> *Jesus knowing that the Father had given all things into his hands, and that he was come from God, and went to God; He riseth from supper, and laid aside his garments; and took a towel, and girded himself. After that he poureth water into a bason, and began to wash the disciples' feet, and to wipe them with the towel wherewith he was girded. (John 13:3–5)*

This is a story many may know, but people sometimes don't slow down enough to catch it fully. When compared to marriage, there may be someone who says, "I'm not going to serve my spouse and concentrate on their needs!" To that, we really need to see something in this story that will break that mind-set.

Let's understand some of the culture of Jesus's time when He was on earth. It was customary that when you had a gathering, especially at the end of the day, the feet of those who came in were washed. The feet were very dirty not only by dust and dirt but trash waste and even animal waste that was on the roads. The feet were usually washed by the lowest-level servant in the home, and if there were no servants, then it was accomplished by the youngest child who was old enough to do it. The important thing to note is that it was always the person of the lowest social standing in the home.

Notice none of the disciples offered to do it. I'm sure Peter thought, *I'm the closest to Jesus. I'm not going to offer.* James and John probably thought, *We're the inner circle of three with Peter; there's no way we will be doing it.* One by one, they all probably thought pridefully, *It's not going to be me.*

I imagine you could have heard a pin drop. I can just

imagine when Jesus got up and started preparing, the faces of the disciples changed, realizing at that moment something they could have never imagined. *This Jesus, the Messiah, the Christ, the Anointed One, the Lord of lords and King of kings, the Creator of everything, the Son of God is actually taking this position of the lowest one to wash our feet!* This is the extreme example of humility, of servitude, and of love. He could have demanded His feet washed, but He did theirs instead. He served.

If Jesus Christ Himself can take the lowest place in the home and meet the needs of others, so should we. In fact, He commands it.

> *If I then, your Lord and Master, have washed your feet; ye also ought to wash one another's feet. For I have given you an example, that ye should do as I have done to you. (John 13:14–15)*

He has given us the example of servanthood, so we can do as He has done.

Living and displaying Christ's humility, servanthood, and love to each other will not only save your marriage but will also make it exactly the type of marriage God intended—and one you have dreamed about.

Decide to Commit to Obey Jesus in Loving Your Spouse

These concepts are hard and challenging and, I have to admit, require change. We don't have the ability to be like Jesus in the way we love our spouses in our own power.

Some of these concepts are going to challenge your thinking and the way you may have conducted yourself for years. It is opening your heart, letting your guard down, and letting gentleness back into your marriage. These things may have been missing from your marriage for a long while. Decide to make that commitment today.

In closing this chapter, I want to share some passages that will give you hope.

If ye love me, keep my commandments. (John 14:15)

This is my commandment, That ye love one another, as I have loved you. (John 15:12)

Therefore, to show love for Christ, we obey His command to love our spouse as He has loved us. Wow. That, in short, is the essence of this book on discovering a new beginning.

Commit to this!

But, once again, you can't do it on your own. To obey a high and lofty goal, to love as Christ does, we need His power to do it. Look at what our loving, gracious, and merciful God does for us.

For it is God which worketh in you both to will and to do of his good pleasure. (Philippians 2:13)

Look deeply at that glorious provision that is from God Himself.

First, we give our hearts and lives to Christ. He then moves into us in the presence of the Holy Spirit (1 Corinthians 6:19–20). Not only that, but it is the same Spirit with the same power of the resurrection of Christ that is in us (Romans 8:11). That's power!

Second, God works in us to will and to do for His good pleasure (Philippians 2:13). When you get closer to Christ, His will becomes your will. In truth, He gives you the want to obey Him. That desire to please Christ will permeate your spirit and mind; you will want to love your spouse more and more. The things you would or wouldn't do that showed a lack of love will start to bug you to the core, and you will want to correct yourself. Realize that is God in you.

The third thing is that God works in us to do for His good pleasure. He gives us His power for action. Therefore, to obey God, He has poured into us His presence, the will to obey Him, and the power to obey Him.

With these, God has removed any barriers that could hinder us from loving our spouse the way He does. We need to be Jesus to our spouse, be Jesus to them first, to love them like He would, to love them sacrificially, and to serve them just like He would.

Decide to commit to this in Christ. Then watch your marriage grow and be blessed beyond measure.

Chapter Eleven

Live Your Calling—Comfort Others

Blessed be God, even the Father of our Lord Jesus Christ,
the Father of mercies, and the God of all comfort; Who
comforteth us in all our tribulation, that we may be
able to comfort them which are in any trouble, by the
comfort wherewith we ourselves are comforted of God.
—2 Corinthians 1:3–4

Let God Redeem Your Story for His Glory

You have been through a lot; divorce and remarriage are
some major changes in life. Remember the Lord will help you
internalize the truths you have read as based on the Word of
God and see it change you and your marriage for the better.
May your marriage be a blessing to you as you pour into it, and
may it also become an example for others who are watching.

No doubt, there are others in your life who have been
divorced. There are those who are thinking about remarriage,
just got remarried, or have been remarried for a while who will
need help and encouragement. Realize, because of what you
have been through, you now have the experience, information
from the Word of God, and the comfort that God gave to you
to now comfort others who are going through it.

You have been through the pain and tragedy of divorce, the rejection of family and friends, and you have thought through the theological issues as it applies to your life. You have experienced hope at the thought of a new love, and you've been through the excitement and hurdles of a new marriage. Realize, others need to know that there is hope, the same hope that you have.

God has graciously walked with you through it all, and as you are determined to draw closer to Christ and each other, your marriage will become everything you dreamed it would be.

Understand there will be days you don't do as well as others; quickly take it to God, make it right with your spouse, and keep working at it with joy. Remember Satan doesn't want marriages to work because it's the example of Christ's relationship with us, the church. Therefore, let Christ grow your marriage and make it stronger with every passing day. Christ can take anything broken and shine His glory through it.

Keep the following points in mind.

Forgive Yourself and Stop Self-Condemning

I need to share one of these moments. There I was, sitting on the floor a few days before Christmas, missing my kids, feeling the longing to be with them and knowing I wouldn't be with them but a few hours throughout the holiday. I was feeling condemned that my kids were going through this, causing them pain. The enemy of my soul was attacking, I was attacking myself as well, and all I could do was sit there crying tears of despair. I cried until my tears ran out and then continued to cry tearless.

Understand, every decision we make in life will affect us; there are consequences. This is the sowing and reaping principle found in Galatians 6:7–8. Understand, wrong decisions by us or others will cause negative consequences, and good decisions by us or others will cause positive consequences. It is important to note that whether it was your bad decisions or someone else's bad decisions that affected you, there are still consequences.

These consequences are what the enemy will use to try to condemn you. The consequences could be the following:

- messing up a lot of people's lives
- missing your kids (You messed up their lives, and they will never be the same.)
- knowing you could have done more to keep this from happening
- the moments of loneliness you feel during holidays or birthdays without your children
- memories of doing things with your children that won't be shared any longer
- the pain if one or more of your children decide not to talk with you anymore or decide to end their relationship with you
- the rejection of family and friends as they feel they need to take sides
- unfortunately, even rejection from some in the church

There are other things that could happen that make you feel condemned. God has an answer for you through these times. In most marriages that end in divorce, some blame can be shared on either side, so for this we have this promise.

If we confess our sins, he is faithful and just to forgive us our sins, and to cleanse us from all unrighteousness. (1 John 1:9)

Understand, if you take any sin to God and confess it with a heart of repentance (willing to turn from sin and turn toward God), then He is just and faithful to forgive you and to totally cleanse you from it all.

You need to realize the awesome freedom of this forgiveness. When the enemy starts to bring up those feelings of condemnation, you truly need to internalize the promise of God's forgiveness that sets you free. You also need to realize this eternal truth:

> *For as the heaven is high above the earth, so great is his mercy toward them that fear him. As far as the east is from the west, so far hath he removed our transgressions from us. (Psalm 103:11–12)*

This means they are gone in God! How far is the east from the west? The answer is it is infinite. God has removed your sin from you—completely!

> *And their sins and iniquities will I remember no more. (Hebrews 10:17)*

Look at the beauty of that promise! Even if you tried to remind God of your sins, He would just look at you and ask, "What sin?"

Let that comfort your heart when the enemy tries—or even you yourself try—to condemn you for your past sins or decisions. God doesn't want you living a life of regret. It's true; things will not be the same, life will be different, but God still has a plan and can redeem your story, whatever it is, for His glory.

Understand you are free in Christ!

> *If the Son therefore shall make you free, ye shall be free indeed. (John 8:36)*

This is amazing and powerful. Sure, you may have moments when those memories and consequences get you down. You may have moments when you feel the strain of broken relationships with children, family, and friends, but know that even though some of these moments will bring you to tears, even heavy tears, you need to remember you are free in Christ.

Also, being in Christ, you are no longer under any condemnation.

There is therefore now no condemnation to them which are in Christ Jesus, who walk not after the flesh, but after the Spirit. (Romans 8:1)

In those down moments, the devil will try to convince you to condemn yourself. The reason is when you condemn yourself, it will keep you from praying or moving on with your life. It will keep you from being the light of Christ because condemnation will keep you feeling unworthy. The enemy wants to keep you down from living the life Christ wants you to live in Him.

If you are living in the Spirit and striving to live in Christ, there's no longer any condemnation for you. When you sin as a believer, God will convict with guilt so that you will quickly come to Him and confess and make things right, but He won't condemn you.

When these down times come and cause you to feel unforgiven, condemned, and worthless, read these verses and memorize them so God can breathe freshness into you in those moments.

When you go through those times, realize Jesus is with you, walking with you, and will never leave you. He knows what it's like to feel alone, rejected, and abandoned. Let Him lift you up and remind you that He is always with you.

Continue in prayer, reading His Word, and worship Him, and your relationship with Him will be fresh and vibrant. Here is a passage that really gives the comfort that He gives.

Let your conversation be without covetousness; and be content with such things as ye have: for he hath said, I will never leave thee, nor forsake thee. (Hebrews 13:5)

There are some important instructions from this verse that are truly helpful for you. The first thing is to let your conversation (conduct) be without covetousness. This means to not live your life always wanting more, especially money and wealth. Many people who are going through troubles believe money will make everything better, but it can make it worse.

The second things is to be content with what you have. This can apply to material possessions but can also apply to the position you find yourself in. Sometimes we aren't content because we hate the situation we are in. Sometimes we can become so occupied with desiring something different that we don't enjoy life or what God has blessed us with. The reason we are like that is that we don't lean into Christ but instead fill our minds and hearts with always trying to change things. We can miss out on what God is trying to do in our lives through the situation.

The third point in the verse is that God will never leave us or forsake us. This verse is one that you really need to take to heart. Once again, there will be times when you will be having a great day and your mind is not on the past, but then suddenly something will happen. A memory will be triggered, and a wave of loneliness from missing your kids will crash over you like a wave of the ocean. Another instance is that you and your new spouse may have an argument and suddenly a fear of this new relationship ending will overtake you. It is in these moments you will need to believe and have faith in the promise that He has not left you. Firmly believing this will keep your mind, heart, and spirit stayed on Christ. The feeling of condemnation and utter loneliness will not truly overtake you, for you know that God is with you, especially in those moments. Knowing you are forgiven, which will help you stop self-condemning will be more easily accomplished when you firmly believe the promise that Christ will never leave you nor forsake you.

Many times, you may feel God is mad and doesn't like you,

because of how others, maybe even some in the church, have treated you. That couldn't be farther from the truth. God loves you and is there with you, no matter how people feel about you, mistreat you, or even reject you. He was there with you through the whole thing and is there in your marriage now, walking with you. Think of that—the King of kings and Lord of lords walks with you, so chin up, child of God. Chin up!

But thou, O LORD, art a shield for me; my glory, and the lifter up of mine head. (Psalm 3:3)

This brings us to the last point of the book.

You Are Christ's Message of Hope

Realize something amazing. You are now Christ's message of hope to others in your friendship circle, family, church, and other areas of your life.

Once again, there are people just like you who are going through or just went through a divorce. They feel like a part of themselves has died. They may be going through feelings of rejection, loneliness, and depression. They may also be dealing with relocating, maybe a loss of finances, and overall changes in friendships, which can cause a loss of self-identity. They need help when dealing with what God says about divorce and how God views them. They need God's help when it comes to dating and remarriage. They need someone to help with the difficult situations of such things as addressed in this book. They need to know that life goes on and can be enjoyable again. Christ can touch them directly, but many times, He wants to use others, and that means you! You have been through it all with the Lord's help, and now you can help others traverse the path that you have walked.

Many in the church and in families don't do this. I remember when I went through my divorce, the worst reactions I got were from other believers in Christ—and, worse yet, from other believers who had been divorced and remarried. I wondered, *Why would people do that? Treat others badly for the same thing they have been through?* One of the main reasons, which my lady and I have talked about, is they haven't fully dealt with the condemnation from their own divorces. Remember from a previous chapter there are biblical exceptions for divorce, and some divorces don't fall into those exceptions. Or maybe they were the offending party that caused the divorce. In the case that they were the offending party and haven't dealt with forgiveness and their relationship with Christ, when someone they know then gets divorced, they may think that person is guilty of the same thing they did. Insinuations go wild, gossip starts, rumors fly, and even though they are believers, they condemn the newly divorced person no matter what. That person should be understanding, which would bring the greatest hope, but sometimes they can bring the worst pain.

This is your choice to decide to be Christ's message of hope. Don't wait to have all the principles of this book mastered; we will all be working on our marriages for the rest of our lives. Decide today, though, to be that light of hope to believers for support and to nonbelievers for encouragement and to point them to Jesus Christ, from where they can receive salvation. Salvation in Christ will bring them the hope they need for life, now and into eternity. You as an individual and as a married couple can carry the call of 2 Corinthians 1:3–4 to everyone you meet who needs the same help.

If your church doesn't believe in this type of ministry, keep at it anyway. You can speak personally into others' lives. Start a home study or even a support group. Continue to discuss it with your pastor and church leaders. Keep it in prayer, and God may open a way to do this ministry in your church as well.

Get a copy of this book and give it to your pastor and church leaders so that they can learn the teachings of scripture on this subject and gain an understanding of the divorced and remarried people attending their churches.

Allow God to use you to bring His hope in others'

situations so their tears of sadness and frustration will become experiences of joy in a new life. May the Lord Jesus Christ richly bless you in your relationship with Him and in your marriage. Be that shining light of hope and help others discover a new beginning—a journey in remarriage.

Printed in the United States
By Bookmasters